BODLEIAN
LIBRARY
TREASURES

REPERT.

DOMI MINA
NVS TIO
ILLV MEA

HOSPES ROGATVS SISTE,
BODLÆVMQVE LOCI GENIVM ET MVSARVM
MECÆNATEM VLTRA CÆSARES AVGVSTVM
QVI BIBLIOTECAM, MOLEMQVE HANC STVPENDAM
CONDIDIT, INTVERE.

BODLEIAN
LIBRARY
TREASURES

DAVID VAISEY

Bodleian Library
UNIVERSITY OF OXFORD

PREFACE

When Sir Thomas Bodley wrote to the vice-chancellor of the University of Oxford in 1598 announcing his intention of founding the library that now bears his name, he expressed the hope that in time to come it would provide 'a notable Treasure for the multitude of volumes'. By gathering manuscripts, printed books, archives, maps, music and ephemera during the four centuries since it first opened its doors in 1602, the library has more than fulfilled its founder's dream.

In the twenty-first century the word 'treasures' is frequently overworked – especially in the world of libraries and museums. In making a selection of a hundred or so notable items from the Bodleian Library for inclusion in a book under that general heading I have chosen some which are undoubtedly treasures and are well-known for being so. No one would deny that description to Magna Carta, for example, or the richly decorated Ormesby Psalter and Hours of Engelbert of Nassau, the copy of St Gregory's Pastoral Care sent by King Alfred to the bishop of Worcester, or the Gutenberg Bible. Other chosen items would strain to fit readily into the category: for example sets of notes kept by civil servants in the seventeenth century (even when those officers were John Locke and Samuel Pepys), or a playbill for a performance of little-known plays at the Drury Lane theatre in 1800, a Lancashire schoolboy's writing exercise in 1813, or a battered and damaged copy of a Russian translation of Charles Dickens's *Pickwick Papers*. All the items included, however, are noteworthy either for the tales they have to tell, the hands through which they have passed, their beauty, or their extraordinary provenance.

Other people would undoubtedly make different choices from among the many thousands of such items in the library. This selection is, however, made by someone who spent thirty-three years on the library's staff and whose imagination has been caught over the years by the items selected. The choice has not been easy but in making it I have been greatly indebted to many members of the library's curatorial staff for advice about areas of the collections with which I was initially unfamiliar. My greatest debt, though, especially in recent years, has been to Janet Walwyn who has turned many of my scribbled draft entries into clean and readable copy.

David Vaisey

INTRODUCTION

The Bodleian Library stands right at the heart of England's oldest university and attracts many hundreds of thousands of visitors each year. At any one time some 65 thousand readers' cards are in operation for those who come from all over the world to read and study the collections that have been gathered over the four centuries of its existence. Alongside these readers are the many more thousands who come to marvel at the architecture of the ancient buildings which house the library and to see items on display in its changing exhibitions.

Four centuries ago in the reign of Queen Elizabeth I, the library's founder, Thomas Bodley (who was later knighted by King James I), could never have imagined the numbers who now flock to his foundation; however, they demonstrate the success of his vision since his aim, as he wrote in 1598, was to found and endow a library which would be 'a notable Treasure for the multitude of volumes: an excellent benefit for the use and ease of students: and a singular ornament in the University'.[1]

Now housing some 11 million volumes on well over 150 miles of shelving, the library has spread to many sites in Oxford and beyond, but its central buildings are without doubt a 'singular ornament'. They occupy an area of no more than a hectare and there and in its outlying parts the visitor may see the work of a galaxy of great architects ranging in date from the master masons of the fifteenth century such as Richard Winchcombe, Thomas Elkyn, Robert Jannyns, John Atkyns and William Orchard – all of whom had a hand in the construction

The first Benefactors' Register

of its oldest building, the Divinity School. They were followed by Sir Christopher Wren, Nicholas Hawksmoor and James Gibbs in the seventeenth and eighteenth centuries, Sir Thomas Graham Jackson in the nineteenth, and Sir Giles Gilbert Scott, Sir Hubert Worthington, Sir Herbert Baker and Sir Leslie Martin in the twentieth. From the end of the millennium the modernist work of the American firm of Kohn Pederson Fox Associates may be seen in the Vere Harmsworth Library which houses the Bodleian's American studies collection and, more recently, that of the British architect Jim Eyre in the Weston Library.

The Bodleian is certainly, too, 'a notable Treasure for the multitude of volumes'. From its earliest days it has attracted benefactors who have been happy to place their collections within its walls for the benefit of posterity, and it continues

to do so. Indeed, in his letter to the vice-chancellor of Oxford University in 1598 announcing his intention to found the library, Thomas Bodley saw as one of his prime duties the obligation to 'stirre up other mens benevolence to helpe to furnish it with bookes'[2] and two years before the library opened he had already provided a book in which to 'conserve a perpetuall remembraunce of every giver and his gift'[3] to his new foundation. Beyond this, however, in 1610 Bodley – prompted by his first librarian, Thomas James – made an arrangement with the Stationers' Company by which the Bodleian became effectively a library of legal deposit (the first of such libraries in the British Isles), and as such it has (save for a period in the seventeenth century) been entitled to claim a free copy of every item published in the United Kingdom. Over the centuries, too, the Bodleian, whenever funds have permitted, has made opportunity purchases throughout the world of individual items or whole collections. The purpose of these acquisitions has not principally been for display but as a 'benefit for the use and ease of students'; and by this the founder did not mean simply students of Oxford University but anyone from what he called 'the republic of letters'[4] (which we might phrase as 'the literate public') with a need to consult them.

This book sets out, against this background, to show just a few from the many millions of important and intriguing items gathered in to the library over the years since it first opened its doors to readers on 8 November 1602, and this short opening essay sets them in the context of the library's growth.

The story of how Thomas Bodley, a graduate of the university and a former fellow of Merton College who subsequently entered Queen Elizabeth I's foreign service, came to refound the library at Oxford that now bears his name is a well-known one. Previous libraries which had been provided centrally for scholars since the university first emerged in the twelfth century had all foundered through failures in security, through changes in ideology (especially during the Reformation) or, particularly, through the lack of an endowment reliable enough to allow a rapid response to a technical development as fundamental as the advent of printing in the fifteenth century. Bodley, during his travels on the European mainland, had observed that for libraries to survive it was essential that they should have both a secure endowment and a continual supply of friends. He therefore set out to make his library what we would now call 'a fashionable charity', prevailing upon his wide circle of friends to support it with books and money. He enjoined his first librarian to widen this circle, and it has been the duty of each successor to the title of Bodley's Librarian (of whom there have only been twenty-five in an unbroken succession) to continue this process. So successful were Bodley and James that within eight years of opening the library it was necessary to build an extension to it, now known as Arts End.

In the library's early years many of those who sent books and manuscripts had lived, like Bodley himself, through the period of the Protestant Reformation when monastic libraries had been despoiled and the books destroyed, and

Duke Humfrey's Library

Charles I by Hubert Le Sueur

they regarded this new library as a safe haven for such things should such an upheaval happen again. In revolutionary times, whether civil or religious, libraries and archives are always at risk. Thus, for instance, the dean and chapter of Exeter Cathedral placed in the Bodleian Library some eighty-one of their manuscripts, including great treasures such as the missal given to them by their Anglo-Saxon bishop Leofric in the reign of Edward the Confessor. Ten years later the dean and canons of Windsor did much the same, giving sixty-seven of their manuscripts. The vice-chancellor of the university at the time of the library's opening made it a present of two volumes of a magnificent twelfth-century English manuscript Bible that had clearly come from the cathedral at Winchester, where he had held an earlier appointment; and the earl of Essex – whose path had crossed Bodley's when both were in the queen's service – presented him with the contents of the library of Bishop Mascarenhas, grand inquisitor of Portugal, whose palace he had sacked in the Cadiz expedition of 1596. Francis Bacon wrote in 1605 that Bodley had 'built an ark to

save learning from deluge'[5], and he was certainly right. During the course of the Civil War, when Oxford was garrisoned first by King Charles I and then by the parliamentary forces, the library was not plundered even though, like the colleges, its coffers suffered because of the king's need for finances, and some of its buildings were used as an ammunition store. Thomas, Lord Fairfax, the parliamentary general to whom Oxford surrendered in 1646, not only put a guard on the library to which one of his enemies, Archbishop Laud, had donated many hundreds of manuscripts from his own collections, but on his death in 1673 bequeathed to it some 129 medieval volumes from his own library.

As the principal non-ecclesiastical public library with a national remit situated in a centre of learning, and before the foundation of the Ashmolean in 1682 acting also as a museum, the Bodleian throughout the seventeenth century attracted, either by gift or purchase, collection after collection of books and manuscripts put together by others. During the second half of the century, however, the agreement negotiated by

Sir Thomas with the Stationers' Company to deposit a copy of every licensed publication had become increasingly ineffective – despite a series of Press Licensing Acts – and it was only partially revived by the Copyright Act of 1710. Nevertheless the library grew, and many of its great named collections which continue to attract researchers from all over the world arrived in the years before and after the Civil War. The collection of 250 Greek manuscripts formed by Francesco and Iacopo Barocci in Crete and Venice was bought by the university's chancellor, the third earl of Pembroke, and given to the library in 1629. Archbishop Laud's gifts of manuscripts (many of which had been acquired by him from libraries in Germany ravaged by the Thirty Years War), arrived in 1635 and 1640. Books collected by Sir Kenelm Digby came in 1634, and many from the library of Robert Burton in 1639. They were followed just prior to the restoration of the monarchy by the huge collection of books and manuscripts made by the lawyer John Selden, for the reception of which the western extension of the original library, added in 1632–37, was renamed Selden End.

Later in the century these were joined by manuscripts from the library of Christopher, first baron Hatton, in 1671; the books, writings, and printing utensils of the philologist Francis Junius followed in 1678; and items from the libraries of Thomas Marshall, rector of Lincoln College, in 1690, and of Bishop John Fell, dean of Christ Church, in 1686. Just as the gifts of William Laud and others had made the Bodleian pre-eminent in the fields of Greek and Arabic, these last three collections provided the materials for the revival at

Oxford of Anglo-Saxon studies. Further gifts, such as those made by Edward Pococke in 1692 and Robert Huntington in 1692 and 1693, added strength and depth to Oxford's oriental collections. The year 1693 also saw the arrival of the books of a former Bodley's Librarian who had gone on to become bishop of Lincoln, Thomas Barlow. Barlow's books were so numerous and so heavy that the shelving erected for them above the original book-presses in Duke Humfrey's Library caused the walls to bulge outwards and might have led to the collapse of the building had not Sir Christopher Wren been called in to devise a series of massive external buttresses. These buttresses remained in place until it became possible to remove them during the restoration of the building in the early 1960s.

By the end of the seventeenth century a solid basis had been established on which the Bodleian could, and would, develop over the succeeding centuries. The library's growth in the first half of the eighteenth century, however, slowed – and probably just as well since, still occupying only the area now known as Duke Humfrey's Library, Arts End and Selden End, it had run out of space. There were hopes that this problem would be relieved by a great extension financed under the will of Dr John Radcliffe, but these were dashed when his benefaction financed instead the building and endowment of an entirely separate library – the Radcliffe Camera – which opened in 1749. Over a century was to elapse before the original hopes were satisfied and the Camera was absorbed into the Bodleian in 1862.

Growth slowed not only because of shortage of space. The

Overleaf: Watercolour of the picture gallery by Joseph Nash, 1809–1878 (Library Objects 702)

Section of the frieze in the Upper Reading Room

foundation of the British Museum in 1753, with its extensive remit and ample space, provided an alternative home for scholarly materials of national and international importance. There may also have been political reasons in that the outlook of many prominent members of the university veered towards unpopular Toryism. In the first half of the eighteenth century, therefore, only the collections of Thomas Tanner, bishop of St Asaph (upwards of 900 printed books and 467 manuscripts) in 1736 and those of the Oxford scholar and collector Nathaniel Crynes (968 volumes) in 1745 stand out.

From mid-century onwards, however, the story is different, both in terms of the growth of the library's holdings and of the storage of them. The top floor of the Old Schools Quadrangle, designed originally as a picture gallery and as a space for the 'stowage of Bookes'[6] was refurbished – its seventeenth-century decor being smartened with the sort of plasterwork and furnishing made fashionable by the new libraries of the Radcliffe Camera, All Souls' College and Christ Church. Fortunately the authorities did not accept a plan to apply similar 'modernization' in Duke Humfrey's Library. A view by Joseph Nash of the picture gallery in the 1850s gives an impression of what it was like. It was not until 1949 that essential building restoration removed the eighteenth-

century redecoration and uncovered a painted frieze probably designed by Bodley's first librarian, Thomas James, as a kind of Jacobean pictorial guide to the library's contents. The elaborate plasterwork which had covered up the early ceiling panelling in the central part of the gallery was removed and reinstalled two floors higher up in the tower, where its beauty remains unseen by visitors to the library. On the first floor of the Old Schools Quadrangle one of the rooms (originally the Anatomy School) was fitted out as additional space (*Auctarium* in Latin) for the Bodleian in the late 1780s, and this toehold was a sign of things to come: in the years between 1797 and 1835 the whole of the first floor was allocated for library use. The rooms on the ground floor were assigned for library purposes between 1845 and 1890. The two remaining rooms in the Old Schools Quadrangle – one above the other in the Tower of the Five Orders over its great gate – have only recently been assigned to the Bodleian. They are the province of the University Archives, which have occupied the lower room since 1634 and the upper room since 1854. Until 2010 they formed a separate department within the university but are now part of the Bodleian's Department of Special Collections.

Great collections arrived to fill these new spaces. Many were placed in rooms named, at the time, in their honour,

while some almost threatened to overwhelm the library by their sheer size. The books, manuscripts and copperplates bequeathed by the omnivorous collector Richard Rawlinson, for instance, which arrived in 1756, formed the largest single donation received since the library's foundation. The manuscripts alone ran to 5,205 volumes, and it was not until 1893, almost a century and a half later, that a catalogue of them was finally completed. Through this bequest the library's strengths were reinforced in many areas, while the Thurloe papers – which form part of it, together with the Tanner, the Clarendon and the Carte collections (the last two of which also arrived in the 1750s) – effectively placed in the Bodleian most of the surviving state papers for the mid-seventeenth century that had either been rescued by the collectors from destruction or had descended to them from their ancestors.

This is not the place to chronicle the succession of collections coming to the library from the mid-eighteenth century onwards. It is enough to point out that while some built on existing strengths, others moved the library – and therefore the research undertaken at Oxford – in new directions. In 1821, for example, the Bodleian – which, in 1664, had discarded its copy received by legal deposit of the First Folio of Shakespeare as out of date (see p. 132) – became the leading British library for literature of the Shakespearean period when it received the collection of Edmund Malone. In 1834 Rawlinson's bequest of 1755 was surpassed in size by that of Francis Douce. Not only was this bequest rich in spectacularly fine medieval manuscripts but its 17,000 printed books included over three hundred incunables. At the end of the eighteenth century both the British Museum and the Bodleian had been in correspondence with the great collector Richard Gough about the fate of his library of books, manuscripts, prints and drawings, and when it came to the Bodleian by bequest in 1809 it gave the library, at a stroke, a pre-eminence in topographical and antiquarian studies on which it has built during the centuries since.

At this time, too, the amount of money available to the library for the purchase of books increased, often through the ability of successive Bodley's Librarians and Curators (the name by which the library's governing body is known) to raise funds over and above its normal income. In 1817 the very large sum of £5,444 was expended in buying the 2,047 manuscripts from the collection made by Matheo Luigi Canonici in Venice (by far the largest purchase since the Bodleian's foundation); and twelve years later £2,200 was spent on acquiring five thousand Hebrew books accumulated in Prague by Rabbi

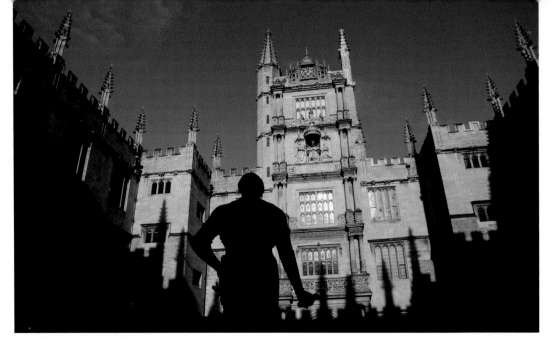

The Tower of the Five Orders

David Oppenheimer, adding enormously to a Hebrew strength stretching back to Archbishop Laud – and, indeed, to Sir Thomas Bodley, who had himself been a Hebrew scholar and versifier. Meanwhile discriminating acquisitions of single books were being made, notable among which was the Bodleian's copy of the Gutenberg Bible, bought for £100 in 1793 from the library of a French cardinal.

Such acquisitions, coupled with a more rigorous application of the legal deposit regulations, exerted unrelenting pressure on the space available in the library's buildings. Throughout the nineteenth century project after project for increasing this space was discussed. The schemes included a plan in the 1850s for removing all the floors in the rooms of the Old Schools Quadrangle and constructing within the shell a huge, free-standing iron stack, top-lit with natural light. This was, mercifully, rejected, as were a plan to roof over the entire quadrangle and another for constructing a second quadrangle in the area between the Old Schools and the Clarendon Building. Among other ideas rejected was one to connect the Bodleian to the Radcliffe Camera by an overhead walkway and an even more radical one to abandon the historic buildings completely and move their entire contents to a new building to be constructed at the junction of the High Street and Merton Street – the site of the Angel, formerly a famous city inn. In the event teaching rather than books moved to that site, into Sir Thomas Graham Jackson's sumptuous new Examination Schools built between 1876 and 1882, but the space thus freed up for the Bodleian's use was hopelessly inadequate. Basements under the new Examinations Schools and the Old Ashmolean building in Broad Street were filled with books, and it was not until the next century that a two-level underground book storage area was constructed under Radcliffe Square (between 1909 and 1912) and connected to the Old Library by means of a tunnel.

Though the librarian at that time, E.W.B. Nicholson, greeted this increase in the space available to him as solving the problem of housing modern accessions for all time, it was never going to be enough – even in the short term. By the

18

second half of the nineteenth century it was reckoned that the library was doubling in size every generation. The number of volumes, estimated in 1885 at 406,159, had by 1915 risen to 1,009,206. A rationalization of some of the university collections that saw pictures moving from the Old Schools to the new Examination Schools and pictures, coins, and artefacts moving to the Ashmolean Museum in exchange for Elias Ashmole's books and manuscripts had done little to relieve congestion in the library. Despite the evident shortage of space, however, many bibliophiles continued to regard the Bodleian as the natural final place for their collections and papers.

The first half of the twentieth century saw the movement of parts of the library away from the central site. The old independent Radcliffe Library, which had moved out of the Camera in 1861 into rooms in the newly completed University Museum, became a place of deposit for some of the Bodleian's science materials, and eventually in 1927 came under Bodleian management, moving into new extended premises in South Parks Road in 1934. A similar arrangement was made with the library of the Indian Institute in Broad Street in 1927. These were called 'dependent libraries' of the Bodleian, and were joined by the new library constructed as part of Rhodes House – the grand building designed by Sir Herbert Baker as the headquarters of the trust established under the will of Cecil Rhodes. This became to all intents and purposes the Bodleian's section covering imperial, colonial, commonwealth and American history. In 1964 the Bodleian's law collections were moved out of the central buildings into a new library

designed by Sir Leslie Martin in Manor Road. Later in the twentieth century the Indian Institute Library was absorbed back on to the Bodleian's premises in 1968, and in 2001 Rhodes House Library was divided into two with the creation of the Vere Harmsworth Library in the Rothermere American Institute. The Bodleian's Japanese collections formed a further dependent library when in 1993 they were moved into the Nissan Institute.

Vere Harmsworth Library

BODLEIAN LIBRARY ~ OXFORD ~ BROAD STREET BUILDING

Sir Giles Gilbert Scott's original design for the New Bodleian Library (Library Records c.618, p.2)

20

Throughout the twentieth century and into the twenty-first, many new directions have been taken in the Bodleian's collecting strategy as the amount of paper-based information has grown (to say nothing of electronic information) and the number of collecting academic institutions – many of which have much deeper pockets – has multiplied worldwide. Magnificent gifts of traditional materials have continued to be made, including, for example, the classical library of Ingram Bywater, the surviving moiety of the library and manuscripts of John Locke, the manuscripts of Percy Bysshe Shelley and J.R.R. Tolkien, the books and papers of Kenneth Grahame, the great Broxbourne collection of bindings gathered by Albert Ehrman, and the outstanding collection made by Dr Bent Juel-Jensen in the fields of sixteenth- and seventeenth-century literature and Ethiopic manuscripts. But at the same time new areas have opened up. The arrival from Oxford University Press in 1968 of the John Johnson collection of printed ephemera, which ironically included some items eliminated from the Bodleian earlier in the century, gave the library huge strengths in support materials for new fields of study. Similarly, the acquisition of the Opie collection of children's literature (part gift and part purchase), when put alongside children's books received by legal deposit in the past, has made the library pre-eminent in that field. The bequest by Walter Harding of Chicago in 1974 of his enormous collection of popular songs (over one hundred thousand American songs alone, for example), together with the transfer to the Bodleian from St Michael's College, Tenbury Wells, following its closure in 1985, of over one thousand music manuscripts gathered by Sir Frederick Gore Ouseley in the nineteenth century, and the donation of the Mendelssohn collection by descendants of the composer in 1960 and 1974, immensely strengthened the library's music holdings. Since the 1960s, too, the Bodleian has with considerable success sought to gather the papers

of modern politicians, and now houses the archives of many twentieth-century cabinet ministers, including the prime ministers Herbert Asquith, Clement Atlee, Harold Macmillan, Harold Wilson, James Callaghan and Edward Heath.

This expansion since the end of the Second World War was greatly helped by the building in the period 1937–39 of the New Bodleian Library. Unlike its sister institution at Cambridge, Oxford did not address the critical space problem faced in the 1930s by abandoning its older buildings and constructing a new library on a green-field site. It debated such a move but in the end decided to keep occupation of its historic buildings and to add another building on the north side of Broad Street, connecting it to the older ones with a tunnel through which ran a mechanical book-conveyor. Though designed following the best available advice for the future growth of the collections and the conditions necessary for their preservation, the half-century of its occupation demonstrated its inadequacy in terms of both space and infrastructure. Its aesthetic merit continues to divide opinion.

Between the Old Schools Quadrangle and the New Bodleian Library one further historic building has in recent times been allocated for library use. The Clarendon Building, erected to the designs of Nicholas Hawksmoor in 1712–13 to house the university's printing presses but vacated by the press in 1826–27 and subsequently used for other university purposes, now houses the Bodleian's central administration offices.

No further expansion is possible in central Oxford, where the historic and rare research materials will always remain. Means are now therefore being employed to store less valuable materials more effectively elsewhere. Outhousing, at the Bodleian as in most other libraries of record throughout the world, is now seen as the answer. Buildings have been constructed, often many miles from the central site, not for their aesthetic appeal or for the comfort of readers but

as efficient stores for items that can be transported either physically or electronically to where readers happen to be.

Meanwhile, on the central site the historic buildings are being adapted to meet modern needs. The underground book-storage area beneath Radcliffe Square now houses recently published material on open access to readers. Known as the Gladstone Link, it can be approached either from the Radcliffe Camera or via the tunnel from the Old Bodleian. The 1930s New Bodleian Library has undergone complete internal remodelling to become the Weston Library, and is the home of the Bodleian's vast collections of rare and important books, manuscripts, maps, music and ephemera from which the items illustrated in this book are taken.

From the many thousands of items which could have been illustrated, those selected have been chosen for their visual appeal or for the stories they have to tell. They are generally presented in chronological order rather than by subject or by the order in which they arrived in the library. The provenance of each is explained in its description.

1   *Trecentale Bodleianum. A Memorial Volume for the Three Hundredth Anniversary of the Public Funeral of Sir Thomas Bodley March 29 1613* (Oxford, 1913), p. 25.

2   Ibid., p.24.

3   G. W. Wheeler, ed., *Letters of Sir Thomas Bodley to the University of Oxford 1598–1611* (Oxford, 1927), p. 7.

4   The words 'respublica literatorum' were used in the inscription which Bodley arranged to be put above the entrance to the Proscholium.

5   J. Spedding, *Letters and life of Francis Bacon* (1868), iii. p. 253.

6   *Trecentale Bodleianum*, p. 72.

TREASURES

A schoolboy's papyrus letter

Some seventeen or eighteen hundred years ago, in the second or third century AD, a schoolboy in Egypt felt slighted by his father and on a slip of papyrus no bigger than a postcard he wrote to tell him so. The letter, subsequently discarded, lay buried until the end of the nineteenth century when, excavated at Oxyrhynchus along with many other papyrus fragments by the Egypt Exploration Fund (now the Egyptian Exploration Society), it was given to the Bodleian Library, in November 1900. Among the literary, legal and financial fragments that make up the other papyri presented along with it, this little document stands out as giving a rare glimpse into family life at that time.

The father, whose name was Theon, was about to go to Alexandria and his apparent decision not to take his son with him provoked the outburst. The letter reads, in a translation from the original Greek by Peter Parsons:

Theon to his father Theon, greetings. A nice thing to do, not taking me with you to the city. If you refuse to take me to Alexandria, I shall not write you a letter or speak to you or wish you good health. So: if you go to Alexandria I shall not take your hand or greet you ever again. … Send for me, I beg you. If you don't send for me, I shan't eat, I shan't drink. There! I pray for your health.

Deliver to Theon from Theonas his son

It is not known if the father's heart was hardened or melted by his son's threats.

MS. Gr. class. f. 66 (P)

26

ΘΕΩΝ ΘΕΩΝΙ ΤΩΙ ΠΑΤΡΙ ΧΑΙΡΕΙΝ
ΚΑΛΩΣ ΕΠΟΙΗΣΕΣ ΟΥΚ ΑΠΕΝΗΧΕΣ ΜΕ ΜΕΤΑ
ΣΟΥ ΕΙΣ ΠΟΛΙΝ Η ΟΥ ΘΕΛΙΣ ΑΠΕΝΕΚΚΕΙΝ ΜΕ
ΤΟΥ ΕΣΑΛΙΩ . . ΡΙΑΝ ΟΥ ΜΗ ΠΑ ΨΩ ΣΕ
. . ΡΟΛΛΗΝ ΟΥΤ . . . . . . ΤΕΝ ΓΕΝΩ . .
ΕΙ Τ . . Α ΠΕΛΘΗΙΣ . . . . ΝΟΥ ΤΕ ΠΑΛΧΑΙΡΩ
ΜΗ . . . ΛΩΣ ΤΙ . . . ΠΙ ΤΙ . . . .
ΤΙΝ . . . . . Ι ΚΑΙ ΗΜΙ ΝΗ ΤΗ ΕΜΑ ΝΕΠΙΣ . .
ΧΕΛΛΑ . . ΟΤΙ ΑΝΑ . . . . . ΤΗ ΕΔΡΟΝ . . ΤΟΙΣ
ΕΑΛΗ . . . ΕΠΟΙ ΗΝΕ ΑΛΛΑ . . ΑΜ ΠΕ . . .
Η ΕΠΑ Α ΡΑΚΙΑ ΠΕΝΗ ΝΗ ΚΑΛΑΙ . . . ΣΕΚΙ .
ΤΗ . . . . . . ΟΤΙ ΕΠΛΕΥΣ ΕΑΥΡΩ ΠΕΛΛΥΟ ΜΗ
. . . ΡΑΚ ΕΤΩ ΕΑΛΗ ΗΜΥ ΗΕ ΟΥΛΗ ΦΑ
Γ . ΟΥ Μ ΠΕ ΠΩ ΡΑΥΤΑ . . . . ΕΡΡΩΣΘΕ ΕΕ ΕΝΤ

ΤΥΒΙ Ι Η

The Laudian Acts

This manuscript of the Acts of the Apostles written in two columns, one in Latin and the other in Greek, is known as the Laudian Acts and is regarded as the most important biblical manuscript in the Bodleian Library. It was given to the library in 1639 by William Laud (1573–1645), chancellor of the University of Oxford from 1630 to 1641 and archbishop of Canterbury from 1633 until his execution in 1645. He had been a fellow of St John's College, Oxford, when the Bodleian opened in 1602, and between 1635 and 1640 he gave the library books, coins and some 1,250 manuscripts in eighteen languages, almost doubling its manuscript holdings. Many of his acquisitions might be termed spoils of war since they had come from religious houses in Germany plundered during the Thirty Years War. This one had come to him from the library of St Kylian's Cathedral, Würzburg, which was dispersed by the Swedish army in 1636, but it was not the first time it had been in the British Isles.

It almost certainly began its much travelled life in Sardinia at the end of the sixth century, where its scribe wrote in a way that suggests he was more comfortable with Greek than with Latin. It may have been intended originally for Greek-speakers less familiar with Latin and is the earliest known Greek manuscript to include (illustrated here) the Ethiopian eunuch's confession of faith, 'I believe that Jesus Christ is the Son of God', prior to his baptism by Philip: Acts 8.37 in the Authorized Version. During the seventh century the book first came to England, possibly brought from Rome by Benedict Biscop (628–690), founder of the abbeys of Wearmouth and Jarrow, for it was there that the Venerable Bede (c.673–735) is believed to have handled it, quoting from it in his two commentaries on Acts. Books in Greek were very rare in England at that time and this one did not remain there. By the turn of the eighth and ninth centuries it had emigrated with Anglo-Saxon missionaries to Germany to find its home in Würzburg until Archbishop Laud's agents acquired it in times of upheaval nine centuries later.

Now the book's importance lies not only in its text but also in its being a reminder of the sources available to Anglo-Saxon men of learning such as the Venerable Bede, who never left his native land, and of the way that biblical scholarship spread through Europe in the second half of the first Christian millennium.

MS. Laud Gr. 35, binding and fol. 70v

The Benedictine Rule

St Benedict (c.480–c.547), regarded as the founding father of western monastic life, laid down a code of precepts for those who wished to live communally. The Rule of St Benedict endures to this day, and the oldest surviving copy of it is in the Bodleian Library. It is illustrated here. It came to the Bodleian in the second half of the seventeenth century and it is the library's oldest book of English origin. It was painstakingly copied from an earlier manuscript (now lost) with corrections by a scribe somewhere in the Midlands of England not much later than the year 700 – a mere century and half after St Benedict's death.

It is more than a rare survival from the beginning of the eighth century. It shows how the rules for monastic life were being taken up and revered by a community in an island off the north European mainland far away from southern Italy where they were first codified. Furthermore, the manuscript is remarkable for the beauty of its script, which blends calligraphic traditions from both Celtic and Italian scribes into a form known to scholars as English uncial. Its bold initials, red edged in black and outlined with red dots, are characteristic of insular book decoration from early times.

It is not known which community of monks in England produced and owned the manuscript, but by the eleventh century it was at Worcester Cathedral Priory. It came to the Bodleian Library, as did King Alfred's translation of St Gregory's Pastoral Care (p. 36), together with over one hundred other medieval manuscripts from the library of the politician and scholarly collector Christopher, first baron Hatton. After his death in 1670 they were acquired by a London bookseller and bought by the Bodleian from him a year later.

MS. Hatton 48, fols 28r – 29r

OEOIRE ETIAM
SIIPSEALITERGO
ABSITACAT·ONE
ONORESILLUOO
MINICUMPRAE
CEPITUM·QUAE
OICUNTFACITE
QUAEAUTEMFA
CIUNTFACERE
NOLITE·NON
UELLEOICISCO
NANTEQUAM
· SITSEOPR
USESSEQUOO
UERNUSOICITUR
PRAECEPTA
FACTISCOTIOIE
AOIMPLERE·A
STPTATEMAMA
RE NULLUMO
OIRE ZELUMET
INUIOIAMNON

HABERE·CONTEN
TIONEMNONA
MARE·ELATIONA
FUGERE·ETSEN
ORESUENERARE
JUNIORESOILIGE
REINXPIAMORE
PROINIMICISO
RARE·CUMOIS
COROANTEAN
SOLISOCCASUM
INPACEMREOI
RE·ETOEOIM
SERICOROIANU
QUAMOISPE
RARE·ECCEHAEC
SUNTINSTRU
MENTAARTISI
SPIRITALIS·QUA
CUMFUERIN
ANOBISOIENO
TUQUEINCES

BILITERAOIMPLE
TAETINOIEIUOI
CIIRECONSIGNA
TAILLAMERCES
INOBISAONORE
CONPENSABILIT
QUAMIPSEPRO
MISIT·QUOOO
CULUSNONUIOI
NECAURISAUOI
UITNECINCOR
HOOMINISASCEN
OITQUAEPRAE
PARABITOSHIS
QUIOILICUNT
EUM·OFFICINA
UEROUBIHAEC
OMNIAOILIGEN
TEROPERECUR
CLAUSTRASUNT
MONASTERIIET
STABILITASIN

CONGREGATIONE

PRIMUS
HUMILIT
OTISGRAOU
ESTOBOEOI
ENTIASINE
MORA·HAEC
CONUENITHIS
QUINIHILSIBI
AAPOCARIUSAO
QUIOEXISTIU
MANT·PROPTER
SERUITIUMSCO
QUOOPROFES
SISUNT·SEUPRO
PTERMETUM
GEHENNAE·UEL
GLORIAMUITAE
AETERNAE·MOX
UTALIQUIOAMA

31

Early Irish Christian art

The Bodleian Library houses a number of early Irish manuscripts, many of which came to it with the collections of Richard Rawlinson in 1755. However, one of the most important came earlier, in the seventeenth century. It is a volume written at the turn of the eighth and ninth centuries which is now known as the Rushworth Gospels (after the historian John Rushworth, who gave it probably in 1681) or, more generally, as the MacRegol Gospels after its scribe and painter MacRiagoil ua Maglini, abbot of Birr, co. Offaly, who died in 821/2.

The leaves illustrated here demonstrate two aspects of its great significance. Opposite is the beginning of Matthew's gospel and shows the very distinctive letter-forms and decoration developed in Ireland during the period when the island was culturally isolated from the rest of Europe, before the Norse invasions of the ninth century. The letter L cut through by a long I begins the Latin opening of the gospel: 'Liber generationis ih[es]u c[hr]i[s]ti filii david fili[i] abraham' ('The book of the generation of Jesus Christ, the son of David, the son of Abraham'). The text is set into a decorative frame.

The leaf on this page contains the text of John 21:16–19, beginning 'Dicit et iterum simon johannis diligis me' ('He saith to him again the second time, Simon, son of Jonas, lovest thou me?') and shows that by the tenth century the book had left Ireland for England, where a gloss in Old English was added between the lines by a priest, Farmon, and a scribe, Owun, whose names are given in the note at the foot of the page. The book thus has the added importance of being one of the earliest surviving manuscripts of the gospels to contain an English translation.

MS. Auct. D. 2. 19, fols 1r and 168v (detail)

An early ivory

This beautiful early ivory panel is set into the upper cover of the binding of one of the manuscripts bequeathed to the Bodleian in 1834 by Francis Douce (1757–1834). His bequest ranks as one of the most valuable the library has ever received and ten other items from it are shown elsewhere in this book (see pp. 64, 66, 82, 92, 94, 100, 102, 106, 114, 128). He also collected ivories. That collection went elsewhere on his death, but this example and one other came to the Bodleian because they were attached to manuscripts.

The manuscript in this case is a gospel lectionary, containing biblical extracts to be read at Mass, for Benedictine use. It was written and decorated by nuns at the convent of Chelles, near Paris, in about the year 800 when Gisla, the sister of Charlemagne, was abbess there. The ivory panel, which may or may not have formed part of the manuscript's original binding, is more or less contemporary with the manuscript although the binding into which it is now set is an eighteenth-century one. It was made in Charlemagne's court workshop at Aachen. The organization of the panel is typical of that workshop and some of the scenes on it are clearly copied from early fifth-century diptychs, fragments of which survive in Paris and Berlin.

The central scene represents Christ triumphant over beasts, as in Psalm 91:13: 'Thou shalt tread upon the lion and adder: the young lion and the dragon shalt thou trample under feet.' The surrounding scenes represent events in the life of Christ, beginning with the prophecy of Isaiah, the Annunciation and Nativity at the top, followed by his childhood and baptism on the right and then by a series of miracles.

A year before his death Francis Douce bought this manuscript with its ivory from the booksellers Messrs Payne, who had acquired it earlier in 1833 in Paris. It cost him £31.10s.0d.

MS. Douce 176, upper cover

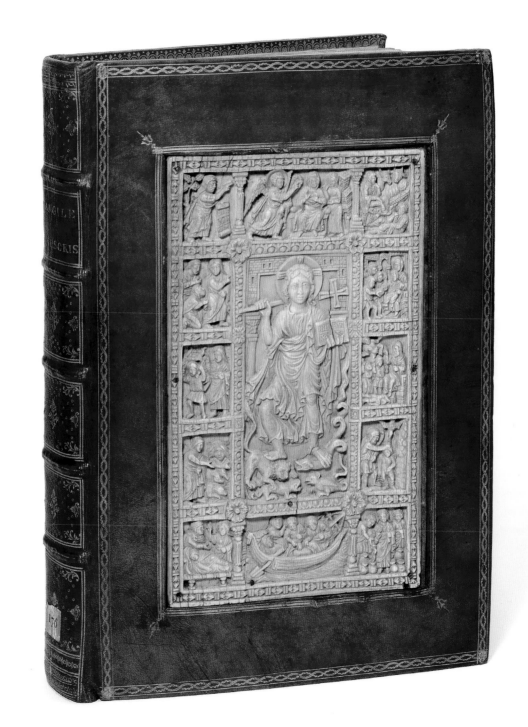

'Alfred had me made'

The turmoil in England in the ninth century led to a decline in scholarship and in the making of books. It was a decline that Alfred, king of the West Saxons from 871 to 899, sought to reverse. In pursuit of this goal he set about encouraging the translation into Old English of important texts previously available only in Latin, undertaking some of the translations himself. One of these was the Pastoral Care of St Gregory the Great (c.540–604), in which the pope set out how a bishop should rule correctly and wisely over his flock. King Alfred sent an English translation of this work to each of his bishops.

Illustrated here is the very copy sent by Alfred, with a covering letter, to Waerferth, bishop of Worcester (d. 915), sometime between 890 and 897. It is one of England's great national treasures since it is the only surviving book that may be directly linked to

Alfred himself. In the covering letter, written in a documentary hand (rather than a book hand) by a royal scribe, the king refers not only to the book but also to an accompanying aestel – a pointer with which to follow the written lines. This links directly to another of Oxford's great treasures, the Alfred Jewel in the Ashmolean Museum, which is now reckoned to be the ninth-century pommel of such an aestel and bears the inscription 'Alfred had me made'.

This volume remained at Worcester Cathedral throughout the Middle Ages. It came to the Bodleian Library, like the Rule of St Benedict (p. 30), from the library of Christopher, first baron Hatton, in 1671.

MS. Hatton 20, fol. 1r

The Alfred Jewel © Ashmolean Museum, University of Oxford, AN1836

P.135.371

✝ ÐEOS BOC SCEAL TO WIOGORA CEASTRE ⠶

ÆLF red kyning hateð gretan Wærferð biscep his wordum lur-
lice ⁊ freondlice · ⁊ ðe cyðan hate ðæt me com swiðe oft ongemynd
hwelce wiotan iu wæron giond angel cynn · ægðer ge godcundra
hada ge woruld cundra · ⁊ hu gesæliglica tida ða wæron giond angel
cynn · ⁊ hu ða kyningas ðe done onwald hefdon ðæs folces gode ⁊ his
ærend wrecum hyr sumeden · ⁊ hie ægðer ge hiora sibbe ge hiora
siodo ge hiora on weald innan borðes gehioldon · ⁊ eac ut hiora
eðel gerymdon · ⁊ hu him ða speow ægðer ge mid wige ge mid wisdome ·
⁊ eac ða godcundan hadas hu giorne hie wæron ægðer ge ymb lare
ge ymb liornunga · ge ymb ealle ða ðiowot domas ðe hie gode scol-
don · ⁊ human utan borðes wisdom ⁊ lare hieder on lond sohte · ⁊
hu we hy nu sceoldon ute begietan gif we hie habban sceoldon · Swa
clæne hio wæs oð feallenu on angel cynne · ðæt swiðe feawa wæron
be hionan humbre ðe hiora ðeninga cuðen understondan on englisc
oððe furðum an ærend gewrit of ledene on englisc areccean
ic wene ðæt noht monige begiondan humbre nęren · Swa
feawa hiora wæron ðæt ic furðum anne anleppne ne mæg
ge ðencean besuðan temese ða ða ic to rice feng gode ælmih-
tegum sie ðonc ðæt we ænigne on stal habbað lareowa · ⁊ for
ðon ic ðe bebiode ðæt ðu do swa ic geliefe ðæt ðu wille · ðæt ðu ðe
ðissa woruld ðinga to ðæm gemetige swa ðu oftost mæge · ðæt ðu
ðone wisdom ðe ðe god sealde ðær ðær ðu hiene befæstan mæge

Hatton . 88 .

St Dunstan

This fine tenth-century image of St Dunstan kneeling and praying at the feet of Christ is undoubtedly the most widely known line drawing in the Bodleian Library, for the consensus of scholarly opinion is that it is by St Dunstan himself.

The leaf that bears it was added at the beginning of a group of four booklets from the early tenth century, three of which were almost certainly bound together at Glastonbury Abbey when St Dunstan was abbot there. He was already known as a skilled writer, painter and musician when he was appointed in the early 940s and, as abbot, he greatly expanded the abbey's buildings and established it as a centre of learning – remaining influential there after becoming archbishop of Canterbury in 960.

The Latin prayer offered by the tonsured monk translates as 'I beseech you, merciful Christ, to protect me, Dunstan; suffer not the infernal storms to overwhelm me.' Christ carries a rod and a book which bear texts from the Latin Psalms: 'the sceptre of thy kingdom is a right sceptre' (Psalm 45) and 'Come, ye children, hearken unto me; I will teach you the fear of the Lord' (Psalm 34). At the top of the leaf a Latin inscription from some centuries later states that 'the picture and the text seen below on this page are in St Dunstan's own hand'.

The drawing is doubly important: as a very fine example of Anglo-Saxon art, and as a self-portrait by an English saint. The volume which bears it is now generally known as St Dunstan's Classbook. It was given to the Bodleian Library in 1601, prior to its opening, by the astrologer and mathematician Thomas Allen (1542–1632).

MS. Auct. F. 4. 32, fol. 1r

The Caedmon manuscript

Among the books and manuscripts that came to the Bodleian Library by gift from the philologist Francis Junius (1589–1678) following his death is a remarkable Anglo-Saxon volume of metrical biblical paraphrases. Junius believed them to be the work of Caedmon (fl. c.670), a shepherd at Whitby Abbey who, thanks to his being identified in the Venerable Bede's *Historia Ecclesiastica Gentis Anglorum*, is the earliest vernacular English poet whose name is known. Scholars now do not attribute them to Caedmon himself but to others, unidentified, writing in the Caedmon tradition and referred to as pseudo-Caedmon. This manuscript, written around AD1000, contains metrical paraphrases of the Old English poems of Genesis, Exodus, Daniel, and Christ and Satan with, on 52 of its 230 pages, illustrations in two different artistic styles in pen and ink.

That shown here depicts the fall of Lucifer – the angel who defied God – and accompanies the paraphrase of Genesis though the story of the expulsion of Lucifer from heaven, is not contained in that book of the Bible. The story is presented in four episodes divided across the page by double parallel lines. At the top the angel Lucifer, crowned, stands as tall as his palace while other angels, some carrying more crowns, make obeisance to him. Below this Lucifer has begun to change, his hair from blond to black, his crown replaced by a laurel wreath. In the third scene a haloed figure, the avenging Creator bearing three spears, threatens him. In the final episode Lucifer is shown twice, first falling towards, and then swallowed up by, the jaws of hell; he has no halo or crown, his hands, feet and neck are lashed to the hellish beast's fangs, and his feet have become claws. His followers and parts of his palace fall with him to destruction.

The manuscript and its illustrations were on display as one of the Bodleian's great treasures in the nineteenth century, when Lewis Carroll (Charles Dodgson, mathematics lecturer at Christ Church, Oxford, from 1855 to 1881) was writing. It is considered by many that these drawings inspired the creation of the messenger in chapter 7 of *Through the Looking Glass* who, with his 'curious attitudes … skipping up and down … as he came along, with his great hands spread out like fans on each side', bore a message from the White King. As the King explained, 'He's an Anglo-Saxon messenger – and those are Anglo-Saxon attitudes'.

MS. Junius 11, p. 3

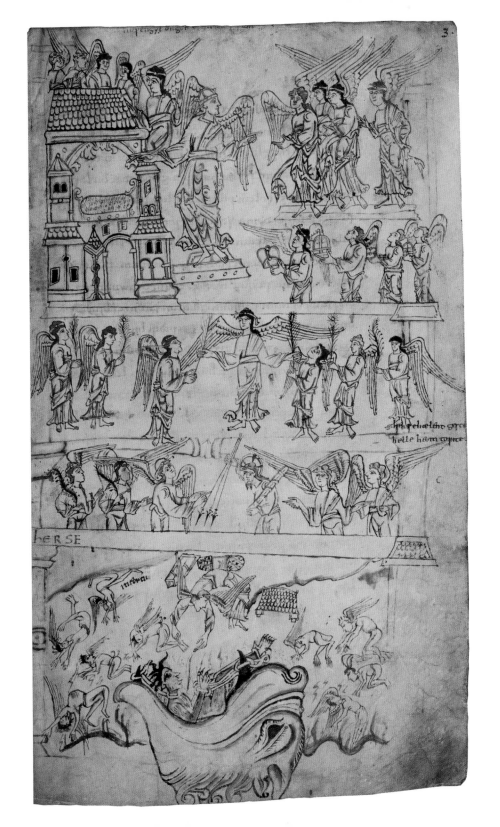

41

A miraculous Anglo-Saxon royal book

In 1887 the Bodleian bought at auction in London for £6.0s.0d. this manuscript which had been misdescribed in the sale catalogue as a fourteenth-century copy of the gospels. It is, in fact, much earlier, having been written and illuminated by the middle of the eleventh century, and it contains only short extracts from the four gospels. It is a gospel lectionary, and it carries at its beginning a poem in Latin that makes it clear that it once belonged to Queen Margaret of Scotland (1046–1093), wife of Malcolm III. Mother of eight children, she was the mother-in-law of King Henry I of England and was respected for her holiness in her lifetime and later venerated as a saint. This little book (it consists of thirty-eight leaves) was said to have been her favourite and played its part in the only miracle recounted in her biography – a Life written some ten years after her death by her chaplain Turgot.

He tells how once when the queen was crossing a ford the book which 'she had always loved ... more dearly than the other ones she studied and read' fell into the rapidly flowing river. It was some time before its loss was noticed, but it was at length found lying in the water undamaged (save for some dampness of the end leaves), even though some small silk tissues, inserted to protect the paintings had been swept away.

Its preservation was regarded as miraculous.

At that time the book had a binding, according to Turgot, 'covered all over with jewels and gold', which it no longer has. Some of the portable relics associated with St Margaret, including a gospel book bound in silver (unlikely, however, to have been this one), were subsequently in Durham Cathedral and were probably plundered at the Reformation.

Its next recorded owner was the sixteenth-century antiquary and collector John Stow. By then it had lost not only its precious binding but also its association with St Margaret. After its ownership had passed through several other hands, it appeared in the 1887 Sotheby's sale catalogue, and it was only after its arrival in the Bodleian that its true identity as the saint's miraculous book was re-established.

It is open to show St Luke, pen in hand, writing his gospel, the beginning of which is on the opposite leaf. The artist, whom some have conjectured could have been a woman, has used a palette of blue, green, yellow and orange-brown. Both leaves shown here are embellished not with gold leaf but with gold paint – remarkably unaffected by its soaking nine and a half centuries ago.

MS. Lat. liturg. f. 5, fols 21v–22r

SCS LV·
CAS·
EVAN
GEL

QVIDEM
MVLTI CONATI
SVT

ordinare· narrationem quae in
nobif completae· funt rerum·
ficut tradiderunt quiabinitio
ipfi uiderunt· &miniftri fuerunt
Uifum eft &mihi afecuto aprin
cipio oma diligenter exordine
tibi fcribere optime theophile·
ut cognofcaf eorum uerborum
dequibuf erudituf ef ueritatem·

Secundum Lucam·

An early Dutch scribble

In 1602 Sir Walter Cope (c.1553–1614) presented the Bodleian with two Anglo-Saxon volumes containing the homilies and sermons of the great scholar Aelfric (c.955–c.1020), abbot of Eynsham. Copied in the early eleventh century, they were later in that century in the library of the cathedral priory of Rochester, Kent. They are very important historical documents in their own right but at some time towards the end of that century an unknown hand (perhaps trying out a new pen) scribbled on the last blank leaf of one of them and in doing so wrote a sentence that has turned out to be of the greatest significance.

He wrote, in Latin, 'Abent omnes volucres nidos inceptos nisi ego et tu', which translates as 'All the birds have begun to build their nests except you and me.' Then, below it, he wrote the same sentence in another language: 'Hebban olla vogala nestas bigunnan hinase hice enda thu.' This is Netherlandish, and until recently has been held to be the oldest surviving written specimen of the Dutch language. Recently earlier fragments have been claimed, but for centuries children in the Netherlands have learned this sentence by heart and have made pilgrimages to the Bodleian to see the words whose survival for nine hundred years could never have been imagined by the person who scribbled them.

MS. Bodl. 340, fol. 169v

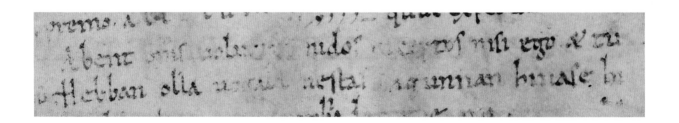

probatio penne si bona sit
probatio in caurx li bonu in

sit orn

probatio penne si bona sit

nostragento quoq; seno.

Iobe... pater nicolae vium dn̄ n
... impietatibus miss deposce.
Scribere qui cupiunt insum... augeba...
Ordare modulos pangamus nobilis modos.
Singula diuisionum... discrimina uocu
... eiono terminat discere... plec...
... metuit formare tenor...
... grauius neus moderando suauis
Apremiul... fide emendo canora
...unus modo cl...
...necis su. nemo a... luua ... quas experimeni u...
Abeint... nudos... nisi ego & tu
... Hebban olla uucu... astai... aruunnan bin... bi...

...geta preter... corles... Hebban olla uucu... aruunnan binase b...

...batio penne si bona s...

Hugh the Painter

This manuscript of St Jerome's commentary on Isaiah is one of the books given by the dean and chapter of Exeter Cathedral to the Bodleian when it first opened in 1602. It was written and the miniatures painted in a religious house in Normandy at the end of the eleventh century, and it is probable that it was commissioned by Osbern FitzOsbern, who came to Exeter as its first post-Conquest Norman bishop in 1072 and stayed until his death in 1103.

The beauty and intricacy of its decoration is shown in the initial letter E that begins the word 'Expletis' on the manuscript's opening leaf. The scene in the lower half of the letter is the burial of St Paula. She founded convents for monks and nuns in Bethlehem and died there in 404. She was a friend of St Jerome and he is depicted in the initial with the Virgin Mary and Isaiah above the burial scene.

The manuscript's last leaf also contains a portrait. It is much smaller and more humble than the elaborate initial with its saints. It is a portrait of someone who lived in the eleventh century and provides us with an extremely rare example of the name and the likeness of a painter who so beautifully embellished the work of the scribes employed to write such books. The tiny portrait is of a monk, tonsured and wearing the Benedictine habit, with a book on a desk and pen and penknife in his hands. Above him are the words 'Imago pictoris et illuminatoris huius operis', ('The image of the painter and illuminator of this work'), and on either side of his head 'Hugo Pictor' ('Hugh the Painter'). He holds his pen in his left hand, leading to speculation that Hugh was left-handed. However, self-portraits are often made from mirror images in which left and right become reversed.

MS. Bodl. 717, fol. vi verso, and fol. 287v (detail, below)

EXPLICIS
VIXEN
GOTM
PORE
INDUO
DECI

PPHETAS UGENI   EXPLA
NATIONU LIBRIS: ET IN DANI
ELEM COMENTARIIS: COGIS ME

Virgo xpi eustochiu transire ad ysaiam: Et qd scs ma
tri tue paule du uiueret pollicitus su tibi reddere. Quod
quidem & eruditissimo uiro fri tuo pammachio pmisi
se me memini. Cumq; in affectu par sit presentia. Itaq; ex de
illi pte reddo qd moneo. obediens xpi pceptis q ait. scrutami
ni scripturas & querite & inuenietis. ne illud audiam cu uiderit.
Erratis. nescientes scripturas. neq; uirtute di. Si eni iuxta aplm
paulu xpo di uirt' e. di sapientia. & q nescit scripturas nescit di uirtut

The Bury St Edmunds Herbal

The medieval herbal was a book with a practical purpose. Its aim was to provide pictures of plants and to accompany the illustrations with notes on the medicinal usefulness of the items depicted. It did not contain original 'research' and, for the most part, the observations had been passed from one copy to another since classical times. By the time this copy was made, its practical usefulness may have been very limited. Certainly many of the representations of the plants had become so debased as to make them unrecognizable – the more so since species familiar in southern Europe in classical times were not so to copyists in medieval northern Europe.

This herbal was copied at the abbey of Bury St Edmunds in Suffolk around 1100 and features in an early catalogue of that abbey's library. It has been conjectured that the scribe was copying from an earlier Anglo-Saxon manuscript (now lost), but ultimately it derives from a Latin original of the fourth or fifth century attributed (in a name borrowed from an earlier writer) to pseudo-Apuleius. Though the Bury copyist may not have recognized many of the plants whose depictions he was copying, he knew what a bramble looked like and may well have painted this one from nature, artistically laying out the design on the page before adding the text.

Its Latin name *herba erusci* is glossed at the top of the page with the English 'a brimbel'. The manuscript was given to the Bodleian Library in 1706 by the eminent physician and anatomist Dr Edward Tyson (1650–1708).

MS. Bodl. 130, fols 25v–26r

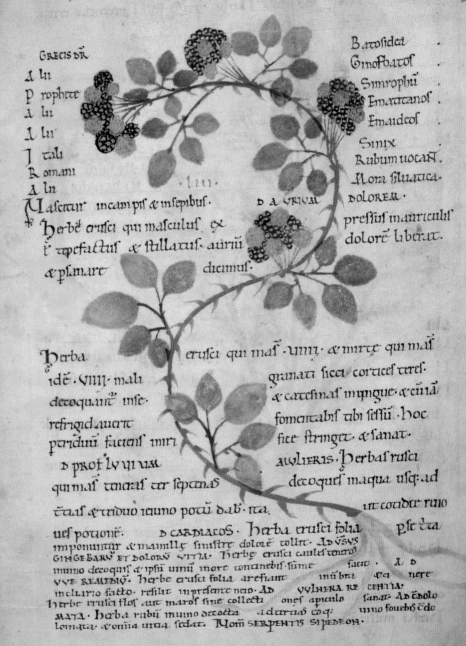

GRECIS DŘ

A lu
P rophete
A lu
A lu
I tali
R omani
A lu

· luι ·

Uascetur incampis & insepibus.

Herbę eruscι quι masculus. &
ī tepefactus & stillatus auriū
& psanare   dicimus.

D A ORIOM

Batosidea   ·
Cinosbatos   ·
Simrophū   ·
Ematcianos   ·
Ematideos   ·
Simix
Rubum uocā.
Rora siluatica
DOLOREM .
pressus mauriculis
dolorē liberat.

Herba   erusci quι maś · uιιιι · & mιrtę quι maś
idē · uιιιι · mali   granati sicci cortices teres
decoquūtꝰ inse   & catesmas im(m)que · & ciuā
refrigidauerit   fomentabis tibi sessū · hoc
pariditū faciens miri   sιcc stringet · & sanat.
   D PROFLUUIUM   AULIERIS · Herbas rusci
quι maś tencras ter septenas   decoquis maqua usq: ad
tdas & triduo ieiuno potū dab · ita.   ut coadιt ratio
ues potιonē.   D CARDIACOS · Herba erusci folia   pset ita
imponuntur & mamillę sinistre dolorē tollit. ADuersus
GINGEBARU ET DOLORIS UITIA. Herbę erusci caulis teneros   sacιιu · A D
muino decoquis & ipsū uιnū more conanebis · sume
UUE REMEDIU · herbe erusci folia aresiant   inūbri   ea   nere
inclario satto · resilit inpresente nero. AD   UULNERA RE   centia
Herbe erusci flos aut maros sine collecti   ones apiculo   sanat AD Dolo
MATA · Herba rubu muino decocta   ad ucriad coq.   uino fouebis & do
lomatu & omnia uιtιa sedat. Uom SERPENTIS SIPEDEON

La Chanson de Roland

One of the great masterpieces of early French literature – indeed a French national epic – is *La Chanson de Roland*. Developed for sung performance by minstrels or *jongleurs*, the poem, or *roman*, tells the story of the eighth-century Christian heroes Roland and Oliver and their death at the hands of the Saracens at the Battle of Roncevaux in the Pyrenees in 778.

The earliest surviving manuscript for the *roman*, shown here, dates from perhaps the second quarter of the twelfth century, and it may seem surprising that not only is it in an English library – the Bodleian – but that its origin appears to have been on the English side of the Channel. The Norman Conquest, three-quarters of a century earlier, had ensured that French became the language of the ruling and educated classes at whose gatherings *jongleurs* would have recited *chansons de geste* such as this, and the manuscript's dialect certainly appears to be Anglo-Norman. The final line of the poem reads 'Ci fait la geste que Turoldus declinet' but it is not known if this was its author, performer, scribe or merely its source. This has led one authority to claim the sentence as 'without a doubt the most frequently discussed single verse in the entire corpus of Old French poetry'.

The word most often used to describe the condition of this historic treasure is 'scruffy' and it is not difficult to imagine it travelling from place to place in the *jongleur's* baggage on the way to a performance. Indications that it was a performer's book are provided by the repetition of the letters AOI at the end of certain laisses or stanzas, either as an exclamation or a refrain, as shown twice on the leaf illustrated – which recounts how the dying Roland summoned help from Charlemagne with a mighty blast on his horn (*olifan*).

Incongruously, it is bound up with a twelfth-century work of scholarship, a copy of Plato's Timaeus, and has been so at least since the early seventeenth century, when both belonged to the Oxford astrologer and scholar Thomas Allen (1540–1632), before being acquired by Sir Kenelm Digby (1603–1665) and given to the Bodleian in 1634. The Latin Timaeus is inscribed as having been bequeathed to Oseney Abbey near Oxford in the mid-thirteenth century and it is possible that the two manuscripts, originating in quite different circumstances, have been together since then.

MS. Digby 23, part 2, binding and fol. 32r

50

ß ire ſtolt y noſ ſer oluer·

p ur deu uoſ pri ne noſ eſcuncaliez·

j al co nerſ ne noſ aureit meſter·

ō aiſ ne pur quant ſi eſt il aſez melz·

Y enget li reıſ ſi nuſ purrat uenger·

j a cil deſpaıgne ne ſen deuret crier luez·

H rē franceıſ i deſcendrūt a pıéſ·

τ ruuerṭ noſ y morz y detrenchıez·

L euerunt noſ en bıereſ ſur ſumerſ·

ß i nuſ plurrant de doel y de pıtét·

e nſuerunt en crreſ demulterſ·

H en mangerunt ne lu ne porc ne chen·

R eſpunt roll ſıre mult diteſ bien· ao1·

oſt ad mıſ loliſan a ſa buche·

e mpeınt le ben par grant uertut le ſunet·

h alt ſunt li puı y la uoız eſt mult lunge·

G rant· xxx· liwes l oırent il reſpundre·

k arleſ loıt y ſeſ cōpaıgneſ tuteſ·

C o dıt li reıſ bataılle ſunt nꝛe hume·

e guenelun li reſpundıt encūtre·

ß altre le deſıſt ıa ſemblaſt grant mençunge· aoı·

ı quenſ roll· par peıne y par ahanſ·

p ar grant dulor ſuneṭ ſun oliſan·

p ar mı la buche en ſaıṭ forſ li cler ſancſ·

þ e ſun ceruel le teple enꞇ rūpanṭ·

ø el corn qui! tient loıe en eſt mult grant·

Unprepared evangelists

In 1817 the Bodleian Library, borrowing money from the Radcliffe Trustees and Oxford University's bankers, undertook the largest purchase it had ever made. It bought for £5,444 the collection of well over two thousand manuscripts amassed in Venice by a Jesuit, Matteo Luigi Canonici (1727–1805). Among them is a copy of the four gospels written and illustrated for the abbey of Ranshofen in the diocese of Salzburg in Upper Austria and dated 1178. Now known as the Ranshofen Gospels, ever since its inclusion in an exhibition in Manchester in 1959 it has been recognized as an outstanding example of Romanesque art.

It is scarcely surprising that so many representations of scribes, painters and writers survive from the Middle Ages. This was, after all, the activity that those who wrote and decorated manuscripts knew most about and it was therefore natural that a text being copied should be illustrated with a representation of its originator. In particular, the four Christian evangelists are frequently pictured at their desks at the beginning of each of the gospels. The Ranshofen Gospels are no exception and the illustrations are particularly interesting, not only as fine examples of the Romanesque style with the use of gold leaf and the way each subject is set in an architectural surround, but also for another reason. The artist has deliberately shown three of the four evangelists as being ill-equipped for their task of gospel writing. Each is depicted with his symbol. St Matthew, seemingly admonished by his angel, sits at his desk with a penknife in his right hand, a leaf of parchment ready and ink in an inkhorn, but has no pen. St Mark, with his lion, has pen, penknife and parchment, but his inkhorn is on the wrong side of his desk. St Luke, with the bull, has two desks, pen, penknife and properly positioned ink, but no parchment. Only St John, the 'beloved disciple' of Jesus, watched over by his eagle, is shown with everything required for writing such an important work.

MS. Canon. Bibl. Lat. 60, fols 14v, 48v, 73v, 109v

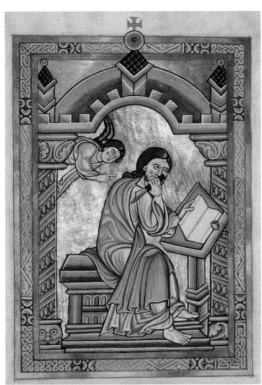

Oxford University's first charter

Britain's oldest university, Oxford, has no deed of foundation. It gradually emerged during the twelfth century as a group of around seventy teaching masters under ecclesiastical authority, with their pupils living largely in rented accommodation in a much older town. Relationships between townsmen and scholars were not always harmonious, and it was a particularly violent episode that led to the issue of this document. Dated 20 June 1214, it is Oxford University's first charter.

In 1209 it was rumoured that a student had murdered a townswoman. In reprisal the town's mayor and other officers went to his lodgings and, unable to find him, hanged two of his accomplices. Incensed by this, the masters shut down the schools and, together with their pupils, left the town. They dispersed to many parts of the country – notably to Cambridge, where a new university began. A settlement of this dispute took five years to achieve because the country as a whole had been placed under an interdict by Pope Innocent III in 1208. The ecclesiastical authorities could not act until that interdict was lifted in 1213, with King John's submission to papal authority. The pope's legate overseeing the rapprochement was Nicholas de Romania, cardinal bishop of Tusculum, and the citizens of Oxford sought absolution from him in order to bring a resolution to the conflict with the teaching masters. This charter, measuring a mere 20 x 11cm and authenticated with his seal, contains the cardinal's settlement. It is known as the Award of the Papal Legate.

Among its provisions, rents charged to scholars were to be controlled, the town was to pay 52 shillings annually for the support of poor scholars and to provide a free dinner for a hundred of them on 6 December each year, prices charged to students for food and other necessaries were to be reasonable, and clerks arrested for any offence were to be handed over to the bishop of Lincoln (in whose diocese Oxford lay) for trial. Thus for the first time the masters and their students were provided with an annual income and in addition the bishop was obliged to appoint a chancellor to be 'set over the scholars'. The term *universitas*, implying a formal corporation, is not recorded at Oxford before 1231, but this award not only increased the standing of the masters collectively within the town but also increased the authority of the bishop over the masters. In the provision of a chancellor in order to exercise this authority, the award laid down the beginnings of a university organization.

OU Archives WPβ /P/12/1

Nichol' dei gr̄a Tusculan' eps Apl̄ice Sedis Legatus: Omibʒ xp̄i fidelibʒ salt' in dn̄o. Unuscuiusqʒ ur̄e notum facim' qd cu̅ burgenses Oxon' p suspendio c̄lic̄or qd c̄omiserant mandatis ecc̄lie p om̅ia stare ur̄aluerint: nos uolentes agere miser̄ic̄ cum eisdem statuim' qd a festo s̄c̄i Michael' anno ab Incarn̄atione d̄ni millesimo ducentesimo q̄rtodecimo usqʒ in decem annos seq̄ntes scolaribʒ Oxon' studentibʒ condon̅ent medietas mercedis hospicior̄um omn̅ium locandor̄um etiam in eadem uilla. mercedis ing̅m taxate comuni c̄onsilio c̄licor̄ ⁊ burgensiu̅ an̅ recessum scolarium p p̄dem suspendium c̄licor̄. Finitis uo p̄d̄cis dece̅ annis: Aliis dece̅ annis p̄xio seq̄ntibʒ loc̄abunt hospicia sic mercede olim ut p̄dem est c̄. xxxx̅. Hec de hospiciis iam c̄onstruct̄is ⁊ uetustis an̅ p̄fatum recessum c̄licor̄. Construct̄is uo postmodum ut c̄onstruenda aliaqʒ p̄ c̄onstruct̄is h̄ in uetusta: arbitrii gener̄or̄ maioror̄ ⁊ gener̄or̄ burgensiu̅ reseruabunt ⁊ p̄ p̄dem in p̄ utriusqʒ decen̅niu̅ loc̄abunt. Comunit̄ qʒ eiusdem uille An̅uatim in p̄petuum h̄abit quinquagint̄ duos solid' dispensandos in usus pauperum scolarium p manu̅ Abbis de Oseny ⁊ prioris s̄c̄e frideswide de ostio Senaltis frie. Hug'. tc̄ Lincoln' eps ⁊ successor̄ suor̄ ut Archid' loc̄i seu offic̄al' ei' dum c̄ancellarius qu̅ eps Lincoln' ibidem scolaribʒ p̄ficiet: scʒ sc̄licʒ qd Uigint̄ sex sol' soluent An̅uatim i festo omni̅um s̄c̄or̄. ⁊ Uigint̄ sex sol' in alio ieiunij. ⁊ hoc faciet comunit̄ p se ut p alium: unde c̄ illis facient̄. p̄ h̄ eundem eadem comunit̄ ut alij unde ipsius pascet centu̅ pauperes scolares in pane. ⁊ ceruisia. potagio. ⁊ uno ferc̄lo piscium ut alterius sin̅gulis Annis in p̄petuum die s̄c̄i Nichol'. ef eps Lincoln' ut Archid' loc̄i seu offic̄al' ei' dum ipe c̄ancellarius ut alias ad hoc ab epo Lincoln' deputate' p̄uidet. iurabunt eadem p̄fat̄i burgenses qd uictualia iusto ⁊ r̄onabili p̄c̄o scolaribʒ uendent. ⁊ ea ut alia nec̄ essar̄ eis c̄arius qm alijs uendi no patient̄. ⁊ qd in solidum b̄r nusionis cues no facient c̄onstruc̄iones ut onerosas: qbʒ c̄licor̄ c̄onditio det̄ioret. Si uo c̄ontingat aliquem c̄licum a laic̄o c̄api: statim cu̅ fuerit sup eo r̄equisit' ab epo Lincoln' ut Archid' loc̄i seu ei offic̄al' ut a c̄ancellario seu ab eo qui eps Lincoln' huic offic̄o deputauerit: c̄apu̅ ei reddent sc̄dm debitam regni ⁊ ecc̄lie c̄onsuetudine. nec aliq̄ in malicia eru̅t in hiis ut alijs. p̄ qd eps iuridic̄o eludat. ut iur̄ sui ut ecc̄lie sue ⁊ aliq̄ minuat. iurabunt dum c̄ r̄quiror̄ de maioribʒ Oxon' p se ⁊ comunit̄ ⁊ qm in eis est. p heredibʒ suis qd hec omia supr̄a fidelit̄ obseruabunt. ⁊ hoc unanim' ql̄ibz Anno renouabunt ad mandatu̅ epi Lincoln' p qr̄ idem eps uoluit cu̅ nuntiu̅ p̄hebet. Cart̄am quoqʒ sigillo comune sigilat̄m sup p̄d̄cis artic̄lis facient p̄d̄ci burgenses ⁊ epo Lincoln' libabint cu̅ uoluit in custodia c̄ommittendam. h̄anc facient p̄d̄ci burgenses ⁊ heredes eor̄ ut etiam honor̄ ⁊ r̄euer̄enc̄ eo exhibeat habu̅dant'. q̄ magis p eos p̄ fuerint dehonestati. Maiori uo q̄ post recessu̅ scolarium irr̄euerent leguer̄unt Oxon': suspendent p tr̄ennium ab offic̄o legendi ibidem. Omn̅e dm̄ q̄ de suspendio c̄licor̄ offensi fuerunt ut c̄onuict'. uenient humil'r ad mandatu̅ epi Lincoln' eu̅ undem fue r̄elaxatum: Ad sepulc̄ c̄licor̄ discalceat̄i ⁊ discinct̄i sin̅ alijs ⁊ palliis seq̄re eos comunit̄. ⁊ ipm corp̄ deferent eu̅ honore ⁊ r̄euerenc̄ ⁊ cum eo sepeliend'. ubi cleric' p̄uidet. p̄ istud q̄ ut p̄dem est a memedrij bagensibʒ: unanim' ⁊ c̄ard comune c̄onfect̄ ⁊ epo Lincoln' libat̄. licentiam h̄abebunt scolares ⁊ magistr' Oxon' r̄edeundi ibidem legendi: except̄is hiis q̄ p tr̄ennium sunt suspensi: de qbʒ est p̄missum. Si uo p̄d̄ci burgenses qd statutu̅ nr̄m ⁊ ipm uolunt minim'. ex tu̅c s̄c̄o se sc̄lne ex c̄ac̄ionis uinc̄o innod̄at'. ⁊ eps Lincoln' ut successores sui eos ⁊ uillam eor̄ r̄educant i p̄istinam suspensionis sn̄tam. Act' Apd Sem̄pl̄ingehām. xii. kl. Jul'.

Magna Carta

Magna Carta, the great charter of English liberties, was sealed by King John at Runnymede in 1215. In order that its contents should be widely known, many originals – each one bearing the king's seal – were sent throughout the country to be lodged for reference in the archives of religious houses. Of these originals only four survive. King John died the following year and was succeeded by King Henry III, who was only 9 years old. In 1216 and again in 1217 he reissued Magna Carta, and this time it was sealed not by the boy king but by the regent, William Marshall, and the papal legate Cardinal Guala. Of the 1217 reissue four originals survive, three of which are in the Bodleian Library. The charter was reissued three times more in the thirteenth century, in 1225 and 1265 by Henry III, and in 1297 by Edward I. The Bodleian possesses one of the 1225 originals, and so of the seventeen surviving thirteenth-century originals the Bodleian has four.

The reissue of 1217 with its two seals is pictured here. This was the one sent to Gloucestershire and kept at St Peter's Abbey, Gloucester – now Gloucester Cathedral. Its history following the dissolution of the monasteries under Henry VIII is not clear, but it came to the Bodleian in 1755 as part of a bequest by Richard Furney, archdeacon of Surrey, a native of Gloucester and a former master at the cathedral school.

The three others all came by bequest (via the Ashmolean Museum) from the Oxford antiquary Anthony Wood (1632–1695), who had acquired a large number of charters and deeds from the archives of Oseney Abbey – where they had presumably been housed during the Middle Ages.

MS. Ch. Gloucs. 8

56

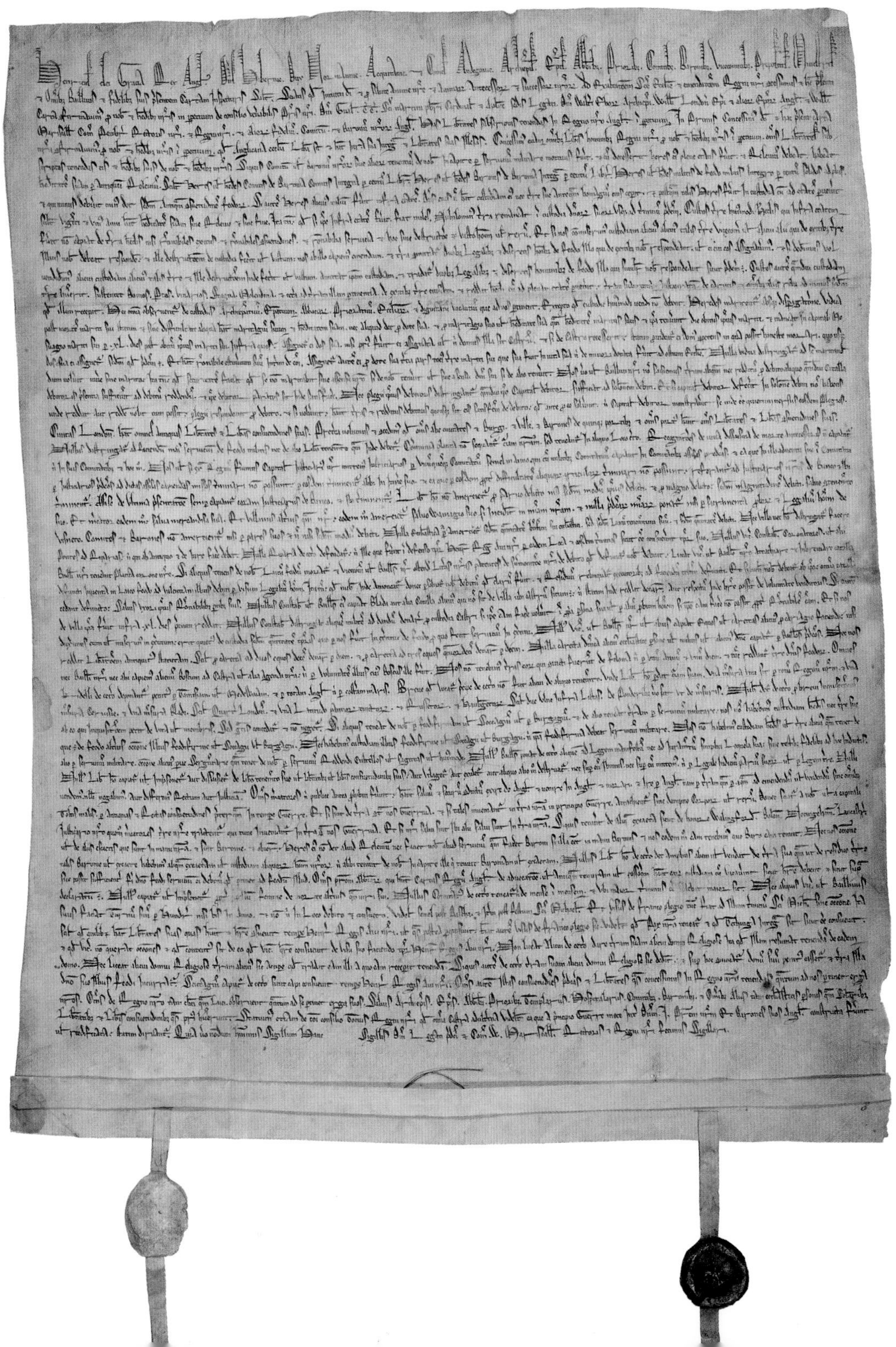

A medieval student's law-book

On Wednesday 12 July 1241 the scribe Leonard de Gopis of Modena finished writing out this copy of the *Decretales* of Pope Gregory IX of 1234. Decretals were official papal letters having the effect of church law. The compilation assembled by topic for Gregory IX became one of the standard collections of canon law studied at the universities of Bologna, Paris and Oxford from that date. The laws themselves were usually accompanied by the commentary of a master – in this case Bernard of Parma (d. 1266) written around the central main text. The result was a very big and heavy volume (this one contains 216 folios – 432 pages – measuring 43cm x 27.5cm) often further annotated, as here, by the student owner at lectures to which it must have been an extremely cumbersome accompaniment.

The leaf illustrated shows one of the historiated initials that begin the five books of the Decretals – in this case the fifth book, which concerns penalties. It depicts a bishop with, presumably, three litigants. This leaf also shows how parchment, an expensive medium, was not wasted even if damaged. Here, and on many other leaves in this volume, a cut has been repaired prior to use by being neatly sewn up with red thread.

The book belonged to William Morris, the artist, poet, and designer, in the nineteenth century. It was bought by the Bodleian in 1942.

MS. Lat. th. b. 4, fol. 168r

Two bestiaries

One of the great medieval picture books, particularly popular in England in the thirteenth century, was the bestiary – the book of animals. A Christianized version of ancient natural history, it had its origins in the Late Antique *Physiologus*, which emerged from the east and was translated from Greek into Latin in the sixth century. It was augmented from the encyclopedic Etymologies of Isidore of Seville (*c.*560–636). Although, however, it emerged from serious scientific works about animals and plants, its purpose in medieval times was not to document the natural world in order to understand its workings but rather to illustrate the Creator at work. Everything was created by God for a purpose and that purpose was the edification of sinful people and to chart the way to their redemption. Few of the animals exemplified were native to Europe and therefore the text greatly benefited from pictures. Many were entirely fanciful, but since they were vehicles for moral tales and precepts it did not harm the book's purpose and for the modern reader adds charm.

The two examples shown here and on the next page are from two very luxurious bestiaries made in England in the thirteenth century. The animals depicted did exist, though it is unlikely that the illustrator would have seen either. Doubtless he would have used his imagination to embellish an image from an earlier copybook.

The whale with its many fins and large staring eye is pictured in a bestiary made in England in the first decade of the thirteenth century. It came to Oxford in the collection of Elias Ashmole in 1692 (the foundation collection of the Ashmolean Museum) and had earlier in the seventeenth century belonged to the two John Tradescants, father and son, botanists and royal gardeners whose rarities Ashmole had acquired. The lesson which it illustrates is that the whale (*belena* or *aspido delone*), stationary and with its back humped out of the water, looks to the three unwary sailors like an island. They stop and light a fire on it, only to be dragged to their deaths in the deep when the whale dives. Thus those who place their trust in the devil will be dragged down into hell.

The elephant, with its erect ears and with tusks emerging from its trunk, comes from a bestiary also made in England, in the second quarter of the thirteenth century. Not as luxurious as the Ashmole manuscript, its illustrations are much livelier and more naturalistic. Its history prior to its arrival in Oxford on, or soon after, the opening of the Bodleian in 1602 is unknown. A companion volume is in the British Library. In this busy picture the elephant is shown as a vehicle of war with, held in place by large straps, a castle on its back full of armed men fighting off a group of attackers who wield

st belua inmari q̃ grece aspido delone d̃r. lacine ũ
aspido testudo. ceꝛ ꝫ dicta. ob immanitatem coꝛ
poꝛ̃ ꝫ qñ fi ille ꝗ excep̃ ionam cuıuſ alıuſ

slings, bows and arrows, swords and axes. The figures
defending the elephant and castle display their identities
by heraldic devices on shields, a banner and a surcoat.
The picture bears no direct relationship to the moral
message accompanying the elephant, which is that it
has no desire to engage in sexual activity ('in quo non
est concupiscencia coitus') until it eats of a tree called
mandragora or mandrake, to which it is introduced by the
female. The parallel with the story of Adam and Eve and
the Fall is clear.

Opposite the elephant is the griffin; which was said
to be vehemently hostile to horses.

MS. Ashmole 1511, fol. 86v; MS. Bodl. 764, fols. 11v–12r

Inter dicta quia inluporum genere nu
meratur. bestia maculis tergo distin
cta ut pardus. s; similis lupo. huius urina
coniti induriciam preciosi lapidis dicitur qui
ligurius apellat. Qd & ipas linos serinis
hoc documento pbatur. Nam egeritum li-
quorem arenis in qnquinum potuerint con-
gunt. inuidia qdam nature ne talis egi-
tio transeat in usum humanum. Ltru dicitur plinius extra unum n admiuet eorum. ista bestia typium tenet inuidos
hominum atqz dolosos qui magis cupiunt
nocere qin pdesse. & iterns cupiditatibz in-
tenti. ea que sibi supflua sunt. & ceteris pdes-
terant. inutiliter seruant.

Gripes uocatur. quod sit animal pen
natum & quadrupes. hoc genus fera-
rum in hyperboreis nascitur locis uel monti-
bz. omni parte posteriori corporis leoni: aliis
& facie aquilis simile. equis uehementer in-
festum. nam & homines uisos discerpit.

Est animal quod dr elephans in quo
non est concupiscencia coitus. Elepha

The Douce Apocalypse

The apocalyptic visions of St John recorded in the final book of the biblical New Testament under the title The Revelation of St John the Divine foretell a series of events that will precede the end of time. This text has been regarded by Christians over the centuries as most sacred – representing a direct revelation from God through Christ to St John.

In medieval western Europe there seems to have been a demand for illustrated texts of the Apocalypse in the century from 1250 to 1350, and especially so in England during the years from 1250 to 1275, with extracts from a commentary by a much earlier shadowy figure named Berengaudus, about whom virtually nothing is known. It is not at all clear why so many illustrated Apocalypses were produced in England at this time (sixteen are known to have survived), but the contemplation of the ending of things may have been prompted by the fear engendered by the invasion of eastern Europe by the Tatars in 1241–42.

This particular example – the Douce Apocalypse – is especially important. Its very accomplished artist or artists are unknown, but the work is unfinished and those pictures that are drafted but uncompleted allow us to see how the original drawings were embellished first by the gilder and then, in several stages, by the painter. Of the book's ninety-seven surviving illustrations (one leaf is missing) thirty are unfinished. It was being made during the years 1265–70 for Prince Edward, the son of King Henry III, who was later to become King Edward I, and his wife Eleanor of Castile. In 1270, however, both Edward and Eleanor went on crusade, and it is assumed that the unfinished book bears witness to the fact that payment for the artist then dried up.

Many of the frequently reproduced illustrations depict cataclysmic and violent scenes involving the overcoming of the devil or antichrist in various guises. This one, by contrast, is of a peaceful scene of the adoration of God and the Lamb, as described in Revelation 7:9–14, by the angels and the elders, and by 'a great multitude, which no man could number, of all nations, and kindreds, and people, and tongues, [who] stood before the throne, and before the Lamb, clothed with white robes, and palms in their hands'. John stands outside the frame of the picture, clutching his book, while one of the elders, appearing at a window, explains that the multitude 'are they which came out of great tribulation and have washed their robes and made them white in the blood of the Lamb'.

The manuscript was bought by Francis Douce in 1833 and came to the Bodleian Library with his bequest in 1834.

MS. Douce 180, p. 20

64

od hec uidi turbam mag
nam quam dinumerare
nemo poterat ex omnibz gentibus
et tribubz zppls et linguis stan
tes ante thronum in conspectu

Et respondens unus de senioribus
dicens michi. Hii sunt qui uene
ru stolis albis qui sunt z unde ue
nerunt. Et dixit illi. Dne mi tu
scis. Et dixit m. Hii sunt q ue

The Ormesby Psalter

This magnificent example of English illumination gets its name from a Benedictine monk, Robert of Ormesby, who gave it to his priory, Norwich Cathedral, around the year 1325. It was written and decorated almost certainly in Norwich by several hands over some forty years from the end of the thirteenth century onwards, but most of its decoration bears the hallmark of one illuminator and has been rightly hailed as a 'superb example of East Anglian art' of the period. It came to the Bodleian in the collection of Francis Douce in 1834, having been acquired by him some four years previously.

Bound in wooden boards and with its edges painted, it has 213 folios and measures 39.4cm x 27.9cm. It still retains the white leather chemise designed to protect it from dirt and dust.

Shown here is the lavishly decorated opening leaf. The tree of Jesse showing the position of Jesus in the royal line of David was designed round the initial letter B that begins the first Psalm 'Beatus vir qui non'. The rest of the text was then painted over with images of the monk and his bishop necessitating a new *Beatus* page opposite.

BEATUS QUI NON

REsurrectio

abit in consilio impiorum 7 in via
peccatorum non stetit: 7 in cathe
dra pestilentie non sedit
Set in lege domini voluntas eius: 7 in
lege eius meditabitur die ac nocte
Et erit tamquam lignum qd pla
tatum e secus decursus aquarum: qd
fructum suum dabit in tempore suo.

A further leaf from this Psalter and images from a third can be seen here. They are those on which begin Psalm 39: 'Dixi custodiam vias meas' ('I said I will take heed to my ways') and Psalm 69: 'Salvum me fac' ('Save me, O God; for the waters are come in unto my soul'). The opening initial of each psalm contains a biblical scene: Christ before Pilate, and Jonah being thrown from the sinking boat and subsequently saved by the hand of God.

The illuminations round the text combine the fanciful with the realistic in harmonious designs – dragons and other grotesque animals as well as recognizable birds and a young woman gathering flowers. At the top of one page a fox disguised with a hood and a walking stick seeks to trick a hare, while at the foot of both pages are examples of a medieval myth and a conundrum. A knight in full armour slays a unicorn which can only be caught when beguiled by a maiden; and a man tries to solve the riddle of how to ferry a wolf, a lamb and a bundle of turnip-tops over a river (in a boat that will take only two of the three at once) and avoid one of his charges consuming another.

MS. Douce 366, fols 55v (details), 9v and 89r

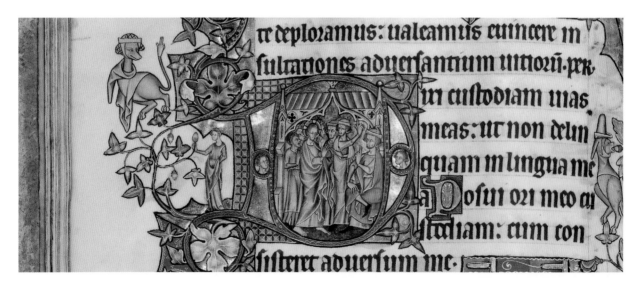

ria feras arundinis congregatio tau
...rum in uaccis populorum: ut excludat
...qui probati sunt argento.
...a gentes que bella uolunt uenie
...ti ex egypto: ethiopia preueniet ma
...s eius deo.
...a terre cantate deo: psallite domino.
...te deo qui ascendit super celum c
...d orientem.
...abit uoci sue uocem uirtutis dare
...riam deo super isrl: magnificentia
...7 uirtus eius in nubib;
...ilis deus in sanctis suis deus isrl
...dabit uirtutem 7 fortitudine ple
...ue: benedictus deus.
...nator domine qui iustis spuale
...epulum tribuis: 7 facis eos ile
...a delectari. concede gregi tuo morte

riam intelligere teq; triumphatorem
mortis: sedentem ad patris dexteram
confiteri. per;

Alvum me fac deus:
qm intrauerunt aq
usq; ad aiam meam.
Infixus sum in li
mo profundi: 7 no
est substantia.
eni in altitudinem maris: 7 tempestas
demersit me.
aboraui clamans rauce facte sunt:
fauces mee: defecerunt oculi mei dum
spero in deum meum.
ultiplicati sunt super capillos capitis
mei: qui oderunt me gratis.
onfortati sunt qui persecuti sunt me
inimici mei iniuste: que non rapui

The Gough Map

Mystery surrounds the origin and purpose of the oldest surviving road map of Great Britain – the earliest map, indeed, to show the island of Great Britain in a geographically recognizable form. Drawn almost certainly in the 1360s, with revisions made perhaps some fifty years later, it is now known as the Gough Map since it came to the Bodleian Library in the huge topographical collection of books, manuscripts, maps and drawings bequeathed by the antiquary Richard Gough (1735–1809). Nothing is known of its earlier history except that he had bought it at a sale in 1774 for half a crown (12½p).

The map depicts England, Scotland and Wales without political borders, and it is drawn in pen, ink and coloured washes on two conjoint skins of vellum measuring together 56 x 115 cm. It is aligned not north and south as is now common but with east at the top and on a scale of about 1:1,000,000. Why and for whom it was drawn is not known, but it seems to reflect the imperial aspirations of the English Plantagenet kings and their territorial ambitions in Scotland and Wales. Certainly England, particularly its south-eastern area and parts of Lincolnshire and south Yorkshire, is depicted with greater accuracy than Scotland and Wales; while London and York (the English kings' administrative centre during the Anglo–Scottish wars) are clearly the most important settlements, with their names written in gold. Altogether more than six hundred settlements are included on the map along with almost two hundred rivers and a network of roads, with distances between settlements marked, extending to some 4,700 km. Features such as Hadrian's Wall are given prominence, as are major rivers such as the Severn, the Thames and the Humber. Large settlements, including Bristol, Chester, Gloucester, Lincoln, Norwich, Oxford, Salisbury and Winchester, are tricked out in some detail. Scotland, a foreign country at the time of the map's compilation, is poorly delineated.

The entire map is a remarkable survival, pre-dating other route maps of the country by some 250 years. Its precision as well as its purpose continues to puzzle scholars.

MS. Gough. Gen. Top. 16. Opposite, from top left: details of London, York and Hadrian's Wall. Entire map overleaf.

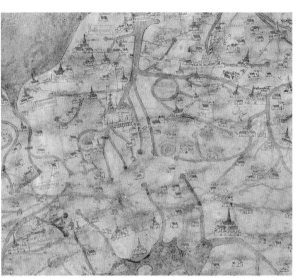

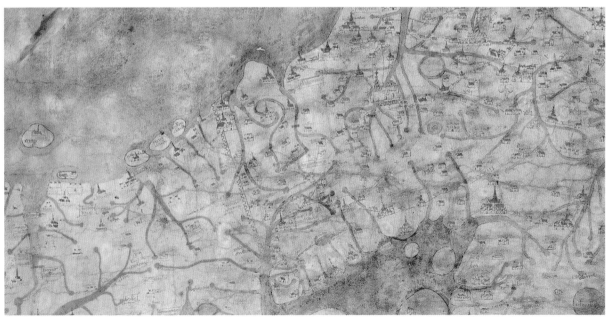

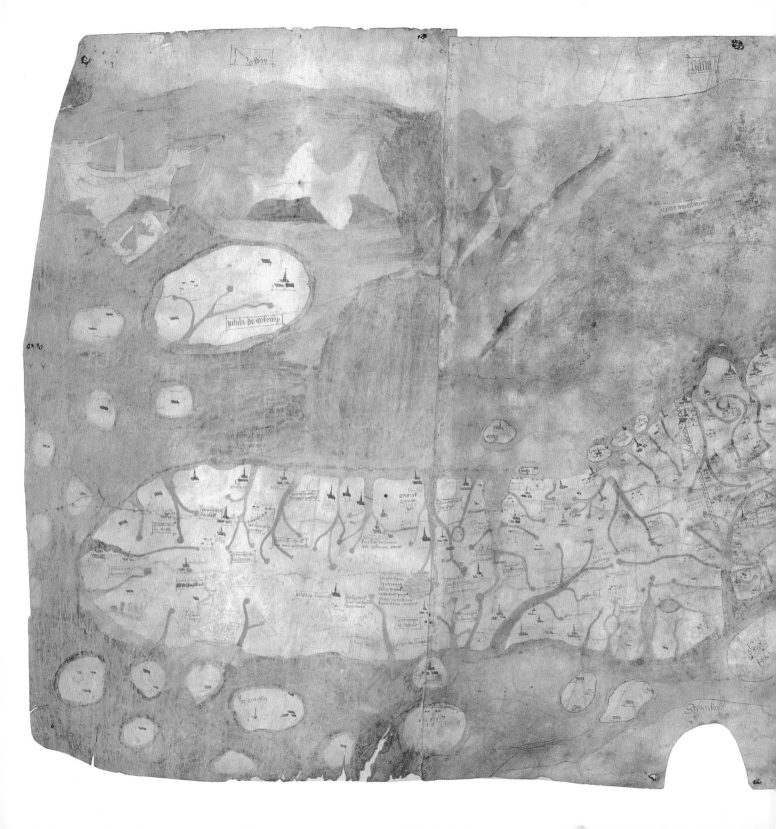

Tales of medieval travel

'One of the great picture books of the Middle Ages' was how M.R. James described the volume from which these two illustrations are taken. It is large and heavy, written in double columns on 247 leaves of vellum each measuring 490 x 295mm, and is profusely illustrated. Speculation surrounds its early history, but it probably belonged to Thomas, duke of Gloucester, who died in 1397, and certainly to Richard Woodville, first earl Rivers, who bought it in London in 1466. It is believed to have been acquired and given to the Bodleian Library by Sir Thomas Bodley himself on or just after the library's opening in 1602 since it does not appear in the Benefactors' Register that he ordered to be kept, but it does appear in the printed catalogue of 1605.

The volume is generally on the theme of travellers' tales and is for the most part in French, which was the language of Romances. The first two parts of the book contain principally a copy of the medieval *Romance of Alexander*, which relates episodes in the life and conquests of Alexander the Great (356–323 BC). The earlier part was finished by the scribe on 18 December 1338 and illuminated by Jehan de Grise, whose work was completed on 18 April 1344. An extra episode, in Middle English, was added by a subsequent owner around 1400.

The first illustration is one of the twelve full-page miniatures from Jehan de Grise's workshop that decorate the early part. It is captioned 'Comment Alixandr avoit vaincu le Roy doire', but in fact depicts Alexander's defeat of Porus, a Punjabi ruler, in 326 BC at the Battle of the river Hydaspes rather than the defeat of King Darius earlier. In the two upper quarters of the picture the two armies confront each other. Alexander, on the left, wears a crown, and a red lion rampant figures on his banners, shield and horse-trappings as well as in the background. Black lions rampant and boars' head devices are born by Porus's army. The two lower quarters show Alexander's army advancing and laying siege to a city, the king himself ascending a ladder. Figuring above and below the architectural frame to these pictures are scenes from everyday life. These scenes decorate most of the leaves of the manuscript and are of the greatest importance for social historians of the fourteenth century. On the roof-line six musicians play wind and stringed instruments, while below a group of youths perform a dance, crossbows are loaded and fired, and wine is poured.

The second illustration – of Marco Polo leaving Venice – forms the frontispiece of the third section of the manuscript, a prose version in French of Marco Polo's *Li Livres du Graunt Caam*, and is one of the best-known images in the Bodleian. It begins the story of his travels with his father and his uncle from Venice to the far east and the court of Kublai Khan between

Tounment alixand auoit daniel le roy dire.

1271 and 1295. The miniatures that illustrate this part
are of an extremely high quality and by an illuminator
working in England about 1400. Written in gold in one of
the miniatures (as if embroidered on the robe of Kublai
Khan) are the words 'Johannes me fecit'. The rest (of
which there are thirty-eight) are presumed to come from
his workshop.

In this scene Marco Polo is seen more than once: on
shore, stepping on to a rowing boat and on board ship.
Behind him many of Venice's landmarks are clearly
shown, including the four bronze horses of the church
of San Marco, the doge's palace and the winged lion of
St Mark on its pillar on the waterfront.

MS. Bodl. 264, fols 51v and 218r

The Agincourt Carol

One of the longest lived of English medieval songs is that known as the Agincourt Carol. Written to celebrate the victory by the army of King Henry V over the French at Agincourt on 25 October 1415, it is still in the repertoire of many folk-singers and the tune was incorporated by Sir William Walton into his music for the battle scene in Sir Laurence Olivier's film of Shakespeare's Henry V, made to cement patriotism during the Second World War in 1944.

It survives in two fifteenth-century manuscripts, one in the library of Trinity College, Cambridge, and the one shown here in a book of musical settings of a group of English medieval carols. Originally separate, this book was bound together with five other unrelated items before it came to the Bodleian Library with the vast collections of John Selden (d. 1654).

The carol itself consists of six verses or 'strophes' with a chorus or 'burden' – in this case in Latin – repeated after each verse. The chorus urges England to thank God for the victory: 'Deo gracias anglia redde pro victoria'.

The first of the verses is written with the musical notation:

Owre kynge went forth to Normandy
With grace & myght of chyvalry
Ther god for hym wrought marvelusly
Wherfore Englonde may calle & cry
Deo gracias
Deo gracias anglia redde pro victoria

The five verses that follow tell of the siege of Harfleur that 'fraunce shal rywe tyl domesday', the battle at Agincourt in which King Henry 'had bothe ye felde & ye victory' and the parade of some of the defeated French nobles through the streets of London, calling on God to give the king 'gode lyfe & gode endynge'.

MS. Arch. Selden. B. 26, fols 17v–18r

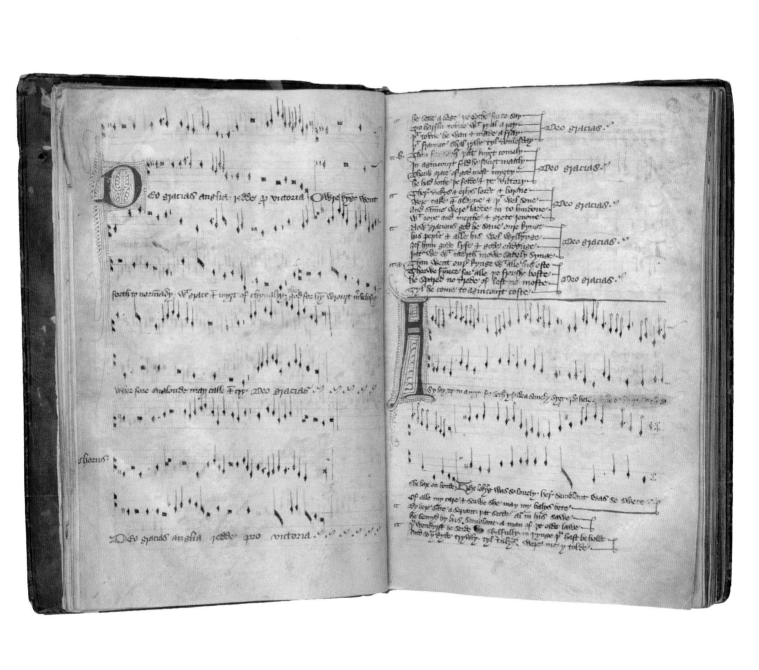

Noah's Ark

Over the centuries the word 'Ark' has been particularly associated with Noah and visualized primarily as a ship. The word, however, simply means a box and in this miniature of Noah's ark from a fifteenth-century Book of Hours it is depicted as such – like a large modern yellow container.

This particular Book of Hours is an exceptionally beautiful one executed around 1440–50 for an unknown English patron by a French artist whose name is also unknown but who is now referred to as 'the Fastolf Master' since another manuscript now in the Bodleian was made by him for Sir John Fastolf (?1378–1459). This one has been in the Bodleian since its opening, purchased, it is thought, with part of the £50 given in 1602 by Lord Cobham. In 1620 John Rous, Bodley's Librarian, displayed it at the ceremony to accept King James I's own works (see p. 146) as 'The Breviary of Henry VII', and there is also a tradition that it belonged to Henry VIII. Both are possible but unproven.

Whether its earlier owners were royal or not, it is lavishly decorated with forty-three full-page miniatures and twelve calendar-illustrations depicting the occupations of the month and zodiac signs. Each of its 264 leaves of text has marginal illuminations of the kind shown here. They are clearly done so that the patterns on the verso of each leaf are mirror images of those on the recto.

This miniature precedes the prayer for peace 'Da pacem domine in diebus nostris' ('Give peace in our time, O Lord'). God is shown against a starry heaven giving a blessing to Noah as the dove bearing its green twig flies beneath the rainbow. From a hatch in the side of the ark two faces peer down at the bodies of those drowned in the flood. No animals at all are depicted.

MS. Auct. D. inf. 2. 11, fol. 59v

Memore de la paux. antiphona

a paxem domine in diebus
nostris quia non est alius qui pu

A beautiful portolan chart

Portolans survive from the end of the thirteenth century. They are navigational charts on parchment illustrating the coastlines and harbours of countries bordering the Mediterranean, later also including the Atlantic coastlines of Europe and Africa. The charts are criss-crossed by rhumb lines showing compass points and wind directions, and are frequently embellished in ways that transform working documents into works of art.

This is a particularly beautiful example produced in Venice in the early fifteenth century. It consists of ten wooden boards, each measuring 29 x 14cm, on to eight of which are pasted seven coastline charts. The last one covers in addition to the northern coastline of mainland Europe that of the British Isles. All are bound up as a volume, with the first and last openings containing four fine watercolour miniatures depicting the Annunciation and the saints Mark and Paul. The style of these miniatures has been linked to the painter Niccolò di Pietro (c.1340–1414). The wooden covers of the volume are polished and inlaid with green-and-white stained ivory and black-and-brown stained wood in a geometric pattern. The whole was fitted into a leather-covered wooden case, now missing its carrying strap, tooled with a floral pattern and with three inscriptions: 'In dio uaner ben', 'per bon amor', and 'per bone respecto'.

It came to the Bodleian with the bequest of Francis Douce in 1834.

MS. Douce 390 and 390* covers, fols 1v–2r and fols 8v–9r

83

A preaching saint

St Bernard, abbot of Clairvaux, is one of the towering figures of western European monastic history. Born into a French noble family in 1090, he joined the Cistercian Order (the White Monks) at Cîteaux in 1112 and only three years later, at the age of 25, established a new monastery for the order at Clairvaux which became one of the chief centres of Cistercian influence and learning. Bernard's own influence, both as a preacher and as a man of affairs, with the ear of successive popes, was immense. He was canonized a mere twenty-one years after his death in 1153. An austere man, ideally suited to an order that practised a stricter discipline than that of the Benedictines from which it had sprung, he was an eloquent preacher whose sermons and lectures were much in demand.

Illustrated here is the opening page of a copy of his sermons on the biblical Song of Songs (*Canticum Canticorum*) made in Florence in the first quarter of the fifteenth century, almost three centuries after his death. In the initial letter V that begins the word 'Vobis', Bernard is depicted at his desk, book in hand and with pen, penknife and inkpot ready for use, either lecturing to or (since he appears not to be speaking) listening to three monks, two of whom also hold books. To his right more volumes lie in a bookcase with a crenellated top. Framing the text in the decorated border six black-clad Dominican friars are depicted, listening, reading or themselves preaching.

Like the Ranshofen Gospels (p. 52), this book was one of over two thousand manuscripts acquired by the Bodleian in 1817 from the collection of the Venetian ex-Jesuit Matteo Luigi Canonici.

MS. Canon. Pat. Lat. 156, fol. 1r

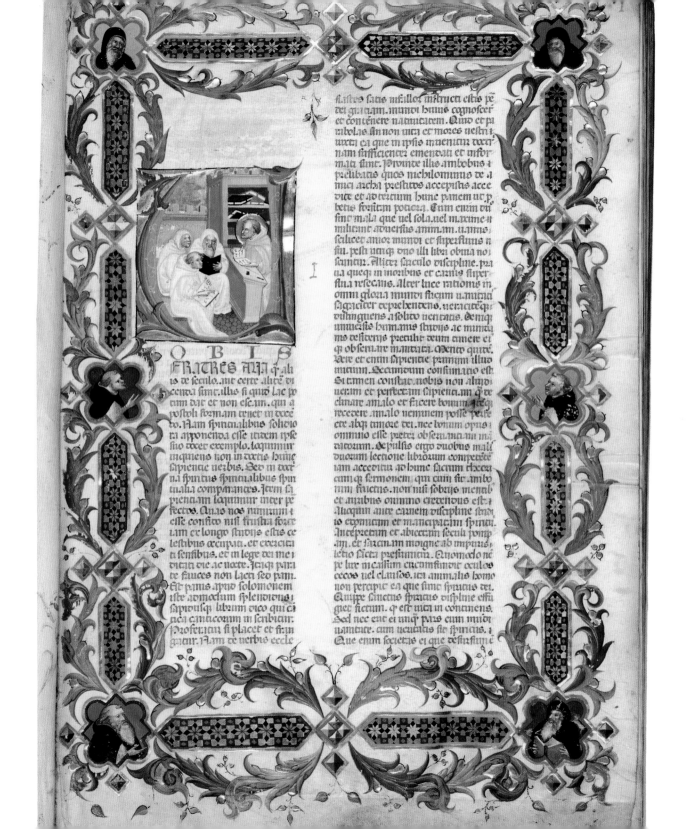

A French view of the Battle of Hastings

This scene illustrates a French chronicle from the downfall of Troy to the death of Charles V in 1380, entitled *Le Mirouer Historial Abregie de France*. The arms and motto of the king's second wife, Isabel de Luxembourg, in the borders of some of its miniatures seem to be additions. It was given to the Bodleian in 1767 by William Bouverie, earl of Radnor.

It is a large book, written on 222 leaves of heavy vellum, almost every one having decorated borders. It also has fifteen large miniatures, of which this is the fourteenth, measuring 365 x 255mm. It depicts the Battle of Hastings after which, as the text beneath it states, Duke William was crowned on Christmas Day by Aerland (i.e. Aldred, archbishop of York). The reader views the scene as if through a large arched window.

At the top, beyond a wood with birds (one of which seems to have escaped into the lower border), boats on a creek and a peasant with a mule, is a fanciful depiction of Hastings. The battle itself is being fought out in the middle and foreground. The Saxons are on the spectator's left. The Norman army, on the right, is depicted as a numerically superior force, with mailed infantry carrying tall red pennants, bowmen and cavalry led on a white horse by Duke William. He carries a lance and a red shield; his surcoat is also red. His opponent, King Harold, crowned and in a blue surcoat, lies dead in the left foreground with a wound in his side and an arrow in his forehead. Alongside him is his lifeless white charger. Duke William confronts the standard-bearer. The standard with its three golden crowns appears again in the scene at the top of the left-hand side of the painting where a kneeling Norman, perhaps William himself, watched by a cardinal, presents it to the pope.

This sumptuous manuscript with its brightly coloured, if stylized, illustrations is clothed in an eighteenth-century binding of crimson velvet with elaborate gilt metalwork ornamenting both upper and lower cover. The whole is protected with a textile chemise of an earlier date.

MS. Bodl. 968, fol. 173r and binding

Oltimodium vero Idem.
Guillermus dux in die natalis domini ab Aelando

The Gutenberg Bible

The Gutenberg Bible of c.1455 is the first substantial book to be printed in Europe using moveable type, and is perhaps the most celebrated of all printed books. It is known that between 160 and 180 copies were produced, but only 47 or 48 survive and of these just 21 are complete. Any library that now possesses one will therefore include it among its greatest treasures. The Bodleian is no exception. The copy which it owns cost it £100 – a fifth of its book-buying budget – when in 1793 it was bought from the library of the French churchman, politician and former cardinal Étienne Charles de Loménie de Brienne. This was at the height of the French Revolution and he died by poison a year later. It is not known where he obtained this copy, but its early history is clear. Its first owner was the mayor of Heilbronn, a hundred or so miles south of Mainz, where it was printed between 1454 and 1456. In 1474 he gave it to the Carmelite house in Heilbronn, and over a century and a half later in 1633 the city of Heilbronn presented it to the Swedish statesman Axel Oxenstierna (1583–1654). At one stage its binding recorded the mayor's original gift, but that was removed when the cardinal had it rebound in its present gold-tooled morocco by the French binder Nicolas-Denis Derome le jeune.

Johann Gensfleish zum Gutenberg, a goldsmith at Mainz who is credited with the invention of printing with moveable type in the west, and his financial backer Johann Fust chose as their first production the Bible in the Vulgate Latin translation. It was a formidable undertaking but it is easy to see why it was chosen. It was an international text and sales could be guaranteed throughout Europe – essential if this initial project was to succeed financially.

Johann Gutenberg pioneered and developed three inventions necessary for successful printing: moulding from lead a succession of identical letters, making an ink that was dense and stiff enough to adhere to metal and then transfer to paper or parchment, and adapting the sort of press used in the wine trade to effect this transfer. The importance of these inventions cannot be overestimated. In enabling identical copies of the same text to be made available over wide areas, his press transformed the spread of learning and enabled the expansion of the human mind.

The Gutenberg Bible brought all these developments together with precision and beauty. The opening shown here contains the end of St Luke's Gospel and the start of St John's Gospel. The black print is embellished with red rubrics and decorated initials added by hand.

Arch. B b.11, fol. 235r

Mane nobiscũ quoniam aduespera=
scit: ⁊ inclinata est iã dies. Et intrauit
cum illis. Et factũ est dum recumberet
cum eis accepit panẽ: ⁊ benedixit ac fre=
git: ⁊ porrigebat illis. Et apti sunt o=
culi eoꝝ: ⁊ cognouerũt eũ: ⁊ ipse euanu=
it ex oclis eoꝝ. Et dixerunt ad inuicem.
Nõne cor nr̃m ardẽs erat ĩ nobis· dũ
loqueretur in via: ⁊ aperiret nobis scri=
pturas? Et surgentes eadem hora re=
gressi sunt in iherusalẽ: ⁊ inuenerunt
cõgregatos undecim· ⁊ eos qui cũ illis
erant dicentes ꝙ surrexit dñs vere: et
apparuit simoni. Et ipi narrabant q̃
gesta erãt ĩ via: ⁊ quomõ cognouerũt
eum in fractione panis. Dum autem
hec loquuntur: stetit ihesus in medio eo=
rum ⁊ dixit. Pax vobis. Ego sũ: noli=
te timere. Cõturbati vero ⁊ cõterriti· ex=
istimabant se spiritũ videre. Et dixit
eis. Quid turbati estis: ⁊ cogitationes
ascendũt in corda vestra? Uidete ma=
nus meas ⁊ pedes: quia ego ipse sum.
Palpate ⁊ videte: quia spiritus carnẽ
et ossa nõ habet· sicut me videtis ha=
bere. Et cum hoc dixisset: ostendit e=
is manus ⁊ pedes. Adhuc aũt illis
nõ credentibus et mirãtibus pre gau=
dio· dixit. Habetis hic aliquid quod
manducetᷓ? At illi obtulerũt ei partem
piscis assi: ⁊ fauũ mellis. Et cũ mãdu=
casset coram eis: sumens reliquias de=
dit eis. Et dixit ad eos. Hec sunt verba
q̃ locut⁹ sũ ad vos cũ adhuc essem vo=
biscũ: quoniã necesse est impleri omĩa
que scripta sunt in lege moysi et ꝓphe=
tis ⁊ psalmis de me. Tũc aperuit illis
sensum· ut intelligerẽt scripturas: ⁊ di=
xit eis. Quoniã sic scriptũ ẽ· et sic opor=
tebat cristũ pati ⁊ resurgere a mortuis
tercia die: ⁊ p̃dicare in nomine ei⁹ peni=
tentiã ⁊ remissionẽ peccatoꝝ ĩ omnes

gentes: incipientibus ab iherosolima.
Uos aũt testes estis hoꝝ. Et ego mit=
tam ꝓmissum patris mei ĩ vos: vos
aũt sedete in ciuitate· quoadusq; indu=
amini virtute ex alto. Eduxit aũt eos
foras in bethaniam: ⁊ eleuatis mani=
bus suis benedixit eis. Et factũ est dũ
benediceret illis recessit ab eis: ⁊ fereba=
tur in celum. Et ipsi adorantes regres=
si sunt in iherusalem cum gaudio ma=
gno: et erant semper in templo lau=
dantes et benedicentes deum amen.
Explicit ewangeliũ scdm lucã. Incipit
prologus ĩ ewangeliũ scdm Johannẽ.
Hic est iohannes euange=
lista un⁹ ex discipulis dñi:
qui virgo a deo electus ẽ:
quẽ de nuptijs volentem
nubere vocauit deus. Cui virginitatis
in hoc duplex testimoniũ datur in eu=
angelio: ꝙ et pre ceteris dilectus a deo
dicitᷓ: et huic matrem suã de cruce com=
mendauit dñs· ut virginẽ virgo serua=
ret. Deniq; manifestans in euangelio
ꝙ erat ipse incorruptibilis verbi opus
inchoans· solus verbũ carnẽ factum
esse· nec lumen a tenebris cõprehensũ
fuisse testatur: primũ signũ ponẽs qđ
in nuptijs fecit dñs ostendens ꝙ ipse
erat: ut legentib; demonstraret ꝙ vbi
dñs inuitatus sit deficere nuptiaꝝ vi=
num debeat: et veteribus immutatis·
noua omnia que a cristo instituunᷓ
appareãt. Hoc aũt euãgeliũ scripsit in
asia· postea q̃ ĩ pathmos insula apo=
calipsim scripserat: ut cui ĩ pricipio ca=
nonis icorruptibile pricipiũ p̃notatᷓ
in genesi: ei etiã incorruptibilis finis
ꝑ virginẽ ĩ apocalipsi redderetᷓ dicẽte
cristo ego sum alpha et o. Et hic ẽ io=
hannes: qui sciens superuenisse diem re=
cessus sui. Conuocatis discipulis suis

in epheso· per multa signoꝝ experimen=
ta ꝓmens cristũ descendens ĩ defossũ
sepulture sue locũ facta oratione· po=
situs est ad patres suos: tam extrane⁹
a dolore mortis q̃ a corruptione car=
nis inuenitur alienus. Tamen post o=
mnes euãgeliũ scripsit: ⁊ hoc virgini
debebatᷓ. Quoꝝ tamẽ uel scriptoꝝ tẽpo=
ris dispositõ· uel libroꝝ ordinatio ideo
a nobis per singula non exponitur:
ut sciendi desiderio collato et queren=
tibus fructus laboris: ⁊ deo magiste=
rij doctrina seruetur. Explicit prologus
Incipit ewangeliũ scdm iohannem.
In principio erat verbũ: ⁊ verbũ erat
apud deũ: et de⁹ erat verbũ. Hoc erat
in principio apud deũ. Omĩa ꝑ ipm
facta sunt: ⁊ sine ipo factum est nichil.
Quod factũ est in ipo vita erat: ⁊ vita
erat lux hominũ: et lux in tenebris lu=
cet· ⁊ tenebre eã nõ comp̃henderũt. Fu=
it homo missus a deo: cui nomẽ erat io=
hãnes. Hic venit ĩ testimoniũ ut testi=
moniũ ꝑhiberet de lumine: ut omẽs
crederent ꝑ illũ. Nõ erat ille lux: sed ut
testimoniũ ꝑhiberet de lumine. Erat
lux vera: que illuminat omnẽ homi=
nem venientem in hũc mundũ. In mũ
do erat: ⁊ mũdus ꝑ ipm factus est: et
mũdus eũ non cognouit. In ꝓpria ve=
nit: ⁊ sui eũ nõ receperũt. Quotqt aũt
receperũt eũ· dedit eis potestatem filios
dei fieri: hijs qui credũt in nomine ei⁹.
Qui nõ ex sanguinib; neq; ex volun=
tate carnis· neq; ex volũtate viri: sed
ex deo nati sunt. Et verbũ caro factum
est: et habitauit in nobis. Et vidimus
gloriã ei⁹· gloriam quasi unigeniti a
patre: plenũ gratie ⁊ veritatis. Johan=
nes testimonium ꝑhibet de ipo· ⁊ cla=
mat dicens. Hic erat quẽ dixi: q̃ post
me venturus est· ante me factus est:

Boccaccio's *Decameron*

Giovanni Boccaccio (1313–1375), one of the earliest writers of Italian prose, wrote the *Decameron* between 1349 and 1351. It recounts how during the Black Death in 1348 seven women and three men met in the church of Santa Maria Novella in Florence, and over the following ten days each told a story a day on a given theme. The entire collection is sometimes referred to as *Cento novelle*.

The artist who embellished this splendid copy of the Decameron in 1467 was Taddeo Crivelli, famous as the illuminator of one of the acknowledged masterpieces of Renaissance book-decoration, the Bible of Borso d'Este, duke of Ferrara. The Este accounts record that Crivelli was employed to illuminate the *Decameron* for Teofilo Calcagnini, a member of the duke's court. The upper roundel on the right-hand side of the richly decorated border carries Calcagnini's personal device of a swan with a knotted and padlocked neck and the motto *li e bien secrete*. The miniature in the lower border shows the young story-tellers gathering in the church. Each member of the group is named and is subsequently portrayed at the start of one day's book of stories in clothing identical to that worn in this picture.

By the seventeenth century this book belonged to the Franciscan convent of Santo Spirito at Reggio Emilia. Its next known owner was Thomas Coke (1697–1759), earl of Leicester, builder of Holkham Hall in Norfolk who, it is presumed, bought it when as a young man he went on the Grand Tour in Italy, in 1714–17. It remained at Holkham Hall until 1981, when along with six other illuminated manuscripts it was offered to the Treasury by the executors of the fifth earl of Leicester in part satisfaction of capital transfer tax. All seven were assigned to the Bodleian Library, where they were reunited with many other Holkham manuscripts that had passed to Oxford in the 1950s to meet earlier death duties.

MS. Holkham misc. 49, fol. 5r

Comincia illibro chiamato decameron
Cognominato principe galeotto nelqua
le sicontengono Cento nouelle in dieci
di recte da septe donne τ da tre giouani
huomini :- Proemio :-

Vmana e la
uere com
passione
ad gliaf
flicti et
come che
ad ciasche
duna per
sona sta
bene ad
coloro maximamente richiesto liquali τ
gia anno di conforto mestieri auto τ ¡no
lo trouato in alcuno. fra gliquali se alcu
no mai nebbe bisogno o gliful caro o
gia ne riceuette piacere. io sono uno di que
gli percio che dala mia prima giouanecza
insino ad questo tempo oltre amodo essen
to stato acceso da altissimo e nobile amo
re forse piu assai chella mia bassa condi
tione non parrebbe narrandolo io sirichie
uesse. quanunque appo coloro che discre
ti erano. et alla cui noticia peruenne io ne
fossi lodato τ da molto piu reputato non
dimeno mi fu egli di grauissima faticha
ad sofferire. Certo non per crudelta de
la donna amata ma per soperchio amo
re nella mente concepto da poco regolato
apperito ilquale percio caminno conuene
uole termine mi lascia contento stare piu
di noia che bisogno nonmera ¡spesse uolte
senare mi faceuan. Nella qual noia τ
tanto refrigerio mi porsono ¡piaceuoli
ragionamenti dalcuno amico τ le sue
laureuoli consolationi chelo porto fortis
sima oppinione per quello essere adue
nuto che non sia morto. Ma sicome
ad colui piacque ilquale essendo egli ¡fi
nito uiue per leggie incommutabile ad
tutte le cosse mondane auere fine. Il mio
amore oltre adognialtro feruentemente et
ilquale nulla forcza dipoponimento o
di consiglio o uiuergogna euidente τ
periculo che seguire nepotesse auea potuto
nerompere nepiegare perse medesimo in

processo di tempo si diminui in guisa che so
lo uise nellanimo me alpresente. lasciato
quel piacere che usato diporgere ad chi trop
po nonsimette nesuoi piu chupi pelaghi τ
nauicando per che doue faticoso essere sole
ogni affanno togliendouia uelecteuole isen
to essere rimaso. ma quanunque cessata
sia la pena non perciola memoria fuggi
ta uebenficia gia riceuuti datuti da coloro da
quali per beniuolenza da coloro adme por
tata. Erano graui le mie fanche nepassera
mai si come credo senon per morte. Et pcio
chella gratitudine secondo chio credo fralal
tre uirtu e somamente da comendare e icon
trario da biasimare per non parere ingrato
o mecostesso proposto diuolere inquel poco
che pme sipuo meambio uicio chio riceuetti
ora che libero dire miposso τ se non ad coloro
che me ataron alliquali peradeunura p lo
loro seno o pla loro buona uentura non be
segni ad quegli almeno aquali fa luogo al
cuno alleggiamento prestare. Et quiuui
que il mio sostenimento o conforto che uo
gliamo dire possa essere τ sia abisognosi assai
poco. Non dimeno parmi quello douersi piu
tosto porgere doue il bisogno apparisse magio
re. siche cio in utilita uisara essi anchora p
che piu utilia caro auuto. Et chi neghera que
sto quanunque egli sisia non molto piu alle
uaghe come che sia gli uomini conuenirsi do
nare. Et se dentro auiluchi pecti temeno τ
uergognanto renghono lamorose fiame na
scose lequali quanto piu di forci amo chelle
palesi coloro che lsanno che lano pronato τ pro
uano. Et oltre aucio ristrette dauolen da
piaceri da comandamenti de padri della
madri de fratelli τ de mariti nel piu del tempo nel
loro circhuito delle loro camere racchiuse di
morano et quasi onose serenuosi uolento
τ non uolento in una medesima hora seclo τ
uolgono diuersi pensieri. liquali non e pos
sibile che sempre strano allegri. Esse per
quello mossa da focoso uisio alcuna malinco
nia sopraauiene nelle loro menti inquelle
conuiene che com giue noia sidimori se da
nuoui ragionamenti non e rimossa sença
chelle sono molto meno forti che gliuomini
a sostenere. ilche negli innamorati uomini
non auiene si come noi possiamo apertamé
te uedere essi se alcuna malincomia o grauecza

S·MARIA   NOVELA

The Hours of Englebert of Nassau

In the catalogue of the Royal Academy 2003–04 exhibition 'Illuminating the Renaissance' this Book of Hours was described as 'one of the great achievements of Flemish manuscript illumination, the most ambitious surviving pictorial cycle by the era's greatest illuminator'. In two volumes since at least the eighteenth century, it was originally one small thick book of some 285 leaves measuring 13.8 x 9.7cm and was made in two campaigns, probably in the 1460s and 1470s. There is some doubt about the identity of its original owner, but it certainly belonged to Engelbert II, count of Nassau and Vianden (1451–1504), and is known as the Hours of Engelbert of Nassau. It later belonged to Philip the Fair (1478–1506), son of Mary of Burgundy.

Shown here is an opening that contains a full page miniature (of which there are eight) and a half-page miniature (of which there are thirty-one). The text is in the hand of a favourite scribe of the Burgundian court, Nicolas Spierinc, while the border and the miniatures are by a master named in the twentieth century as the Master of Mary of Burgundy but now called the Vienna Master of Mary of Burgundy. The miniatures depict the Virgin Mary being greeted by her cousin Elizabeth, in a balmy spring landscape with a pond and water lilies in the foreground and a castle in the background. Opposite it, in a cold wintry setting, Mary and Joseph are turned away from the inn in Bethlehem, with the ox and the ass looking on. Both incidents are framed in a gold border which appears by trompe l'oeil to have resting on it acanthus leaves, flowers and, for the spring scene, a butterfly. This was a technique developed by this particular master and it is demonstrated again and again throughout these two exquisite volumes. Like many of the Bodleian's finest illuminated manuscripts, this one came with the bequest of Francis Douce in 1834.

MSS. Douce 219–20, fols 114v–115r

Margaret of York

This is a painting of Margaret of York, duchess of Burgundy (1446–1503), at prayer with two ladies-in-waiting, watched by an elegant, if languid, young man who may be her husband, Duke Charles. It is one of four superb half-page miniatures that adorn a collection of moral and religious treatises written out for Margaret herself by David Aubert at Ghent and finished in 1475. The volume came to the Bodleian by bequest from Francis Douce in 1834.

Margaret, the sister of the Yorkist King Edward IV of England, was noted for her piety and for her patronage of artists and painters. Among those at her court, too, was William Caxton, who brought printing to England. She was, further, a considerable power in Europe both before and after the death in 1477 of her husband Charles the Bold, duke of Burgundy, whom she had married as his third wife in 1468. Following the deaths in England of her brothers Edward IV and Richard III she intrigued against the Tudor King Henry VII. After the death of her husband she was an active supporter of his only daughter, Mary, duchess of Burgundy, and her husband the Emperor Maximilian I, both of whom also patronized artists and painters.

Although we know the name of the scribe who wrote out the texts, we do not know that of the extraordinarily accomplished painter of the serene grisaille miniature that accompanies *Les douze fleurs de tribulation* (the twelve flowers of tribulation). Over the years it has been attributed on stylistic grounds to various artists whose individual names are not known but whose work survives in manuscripts made for others and who are thus identified by their patrons – notably the Vienna Master of Mary of Burgundy and the Master of the First Prayer Book of Maximilian. Whatever the artist's name, this was clearly an illustrator of the very first rank.

MS. Douce 365, fol. 115r

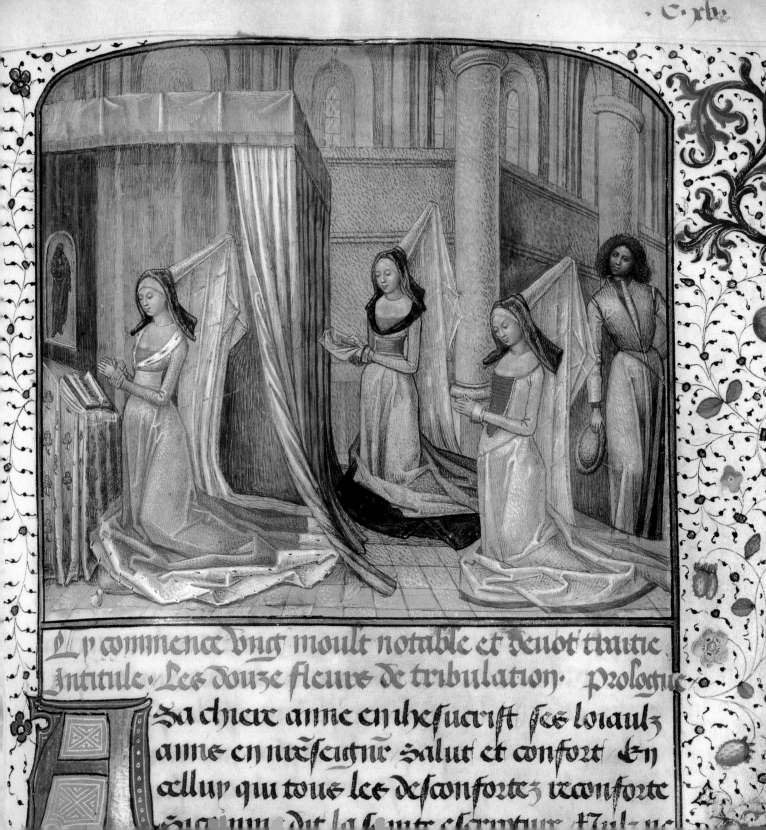

Cy commence vng moult notable et denot traitie
Intitule · Les douze fleurs de tribulation · Prologue

Sa chiere anne en ihesucrist ses loiaulz
anne en miesseigñr salut et confort En
cellup qui tous les desconfortez reconforte
sieamm dit la sainte esaiptur Nul ne

The Kennicott Bible

The Bodleian Library's founder, Sir Thomas Bodley, was noted for his knowledge of Hebrew and encouraged the acquisition of books in that language. The library as a result is now rich in Hebrew books and manuscripts, among which is one of its greatest treasures, the fifteenth-century Kennicott Bible, regarded by many as the most exquisite of all Hebrew Bibles.

Its origins lie in Spain, where it was written, annotated and provided with vocalization marks by Moses Ibn Zabara for Isaac, son of Don Solomon de Braga. It was completed at La Coruña in Galicia on 24 July 1476. This information is given in a colophon by the scribe, while a second extraordinary zoomorphic and anthropomorphic colophon by the illustrator, shown here (fol. 447r), states that 'I, Joseph Ibn Hayyim, illustrated this volume and completed it.' Both scribe and artist were extremely accomplished and evidently worked closely together on the layout of the pages. Well over a quarter of the manuscript's 450 fine vellum leaves bear some decoration and seventy-seven of them are fully decorated. Among the latter a group of 'carpet' pages that divide the Bible into its three main sections bear no text and, like fol. 352v shown overleaf, demonstrate clearly influences from both eastern and Celtic traditions. In only two places is there a relationship between the subject-matter of the text and the decoration, one of

which depicts an elderly King David at the beginning of the first book of Kings (fol. 185r), possibly derived from an image in a set of playing cards. The lavishness of this complete Hebrew Old Testament is unparalleled. Its box-binding of reddish-brown morocco over wooden boards with blind-tooled decoration is contemporary with it. The book also contains Rabbi David Kimchi's grammatical treatise *Sefer Mikhlol*.

Virtually nothing of the book's history is known after the expulsion of the Jews from Spain in 1492 until it was acquired for the Radcliffe Library in 1771 at the suggestion of the keeper of the library, Dr Benjamin Kennicott (1718–1783), who was at work on his edition of the Hebrew Old Testament. It was transferred to the Bodleian Library in 1872.

MS. Kennicott 1, fols 185r (detail), 447r, 352v and binding (overleaf)

Pliny's Natural History

The sumptuous decoration of books for the wealthy was an art form carried over from the era of manuscripts to that of print, and there are few printed books more sublimely decorated than this copy of Pliny's Natural History printed in Venice by Nicolaus Jenson in 1476. The circumstances of its creation are known in detail. The brothers Filippo and Lorenzo Strozzi, bankers and merchants in Florence, paid 50 gold florins to Cristoforo Landino for the use of a translation into Italian of Pliny's work which he had already made for King Ferdinand I of Naples. They then commissioned Jenson to print 1,023 copies (1,000 on paper and the remainder on parchment) and marketed them in various Italian centres, in Bruges and in London; they retailed at 7 florins each.

This copy is one of those printed on parchment and was specially bound and illuminated for Filippo Strozzi (1428–1491) himself by the Florentine illuminator Monte di Giovanni di Miniato (1448–1529). He took four years to complete the exquisite illumination and binding and was paid 76 florins, 15 soldi and 11 denars. The magnificently decorated opening leaf depicts Pliny himself in the initial letter D as a scientific scholar seated at his desk. At the lower left margin is the king of Naples and at lower right Filippo Strozzi and his son. Between the two portraits are the Strozzi arms and two representations of the lamb – the family emblem – with the motto *Mitis Esto* (Be kind). Each of the thirty-seven books in Pliny's work begins with a fine illuminated initial, and in that which begins Book 35 a portrait artist is depicted at work. The whole volume is bound in olive-green goatskin over wooden boards with silver catches bearing the Strozzi arms and those of the Nobili family, who owned the book in the sixteenth century.

Its subsequent history is unknown until it passed into the hands of Francis Douce. It came to the Bodleian with his bequest in 1834.

LIBRO PRIMO DELLA NATVRALE HISTORIA DI C.
PLINIO SECONDO TRADOCTA IN LINGVA FIOREN
TINA PER CHRISTOPHORO LANDINO FIORENTI
NO AL SERENISSIMO FERDINANDO RE DI NAPOLI.
PREFATIONE

ITERMINAI O GIOCONDISSIMO imperadore con epistola forse di troppa licétia narrarti elibri della historia naturale: opera nouella alle muse romane: nata apresso di me nel lultima genitura. Sia adunq; questa prefatióe uerissima di te métre che gia inuecchia nel grádissimo tuo padre: per che usando el uerso di Catullo mio compatriota tu soleui pure stimare qualche chosa le mie ciácie. Tu conosci questa castrense & militare parola. Et lui chome tu sai mutando le prime syllabe si fece alquanto piu duro che non uolea essere stimato da tuoi familiari & serui. Per questo adunq; ditermi nai scriuerti: & áchora per che le nostre chose apparischino & sieno manifeste p questa mia audacia maxime dolédoti tu che pel passato non lhabbi facto in una altra nostra procace epistola. Et accio che tutti glhuomini sappino quanto di pari lomperio techo uiua: Tu elquale hai triomphato & se stato censore & sei uolte cósolo & participe del la tribunitia potesta: Se stato prefecto del pretorio:ilche hai facto piu nobile che tutti glaltri magistrati:perche per piacere a tuo padre & allordine equestre lacceptasti: Et tutte queste cose per rispecto della republica hai facto: Et me chome nel contubernio castrense tractasti. Et certo niéte ha mutato inte lamplitudine & grandezza della tua fortuna:se non che tanto piu possi & uogla giouare:quáto quella e maggiore. Adúq; béche a tutti glaltri huomini sia aperta la uia a impetrare ogni chosa da te uenerádoti: Niente di meno solo laudacia fa che io piu familiarmente te honori. Questa audacia adunq; imputerai a te medesimo:& a te medesimo nel nostro fallo perdonerai. Io mi stroppicciai la faccia:& niente di meno nessuno proficto ho facto: perche per unaltra uia mappansti grande:& di lontano mi rimuoui con le faccelline del tuo ingegno. Et certo in nexuno piu sfolgora quella:laquale piu ueramente e decta in te che in altri for za deloquentia. In te e quella facundia nella tribunitia potesta si conuiene:Con qta risonantia tuoni tu le laude paterne? Có quanta(non sanza amore)dimostri quelle di tuo fratello?Quanto se excellente & sublime nella poetica faculta? O gran fecondita danimo. Certo hai trouato inche modo possi imitare tuo fratello. Ma queste chose chi potrebbe sanza paura considerare: hauendo a uenire al giudicio dellongegno tuo: maxime essendo quello dame prouocato? Certamente non sono in simile conditione quegli che publicano alchuno libro:& quegli che ate glintitolano. Impero che se io publicassi & non lo intitolassi ate:potrei dire perche leggi tu queste chose o imperadore:lequali sono scripte albasso uulgo & alla turba de glagricultori & de glar tefici & a quegli che cósumano elloro otio negli studii?Perche adunq; ti fa tu giudice: concio sia che quando io scriueuo questa opera:non thaueuo posto nella tauola doue sono descripti egiudici:et eri di tanta excellentia:che non stimauo che tu ti degnassi scendere si basso?Preterea quando bene non fussi in si excelso grado:nientedimeno gli scriptori comunemente fuggono el giudicio de docti. Questo fa Cicerone:elquale e di tanta eloquentia:che puo sottomettere longegno al giuocho della fortuna : & quel

The earliest printed advertisement in English

With advertising now all pervasive, it is revealing to observe its origin in England. This small slip of paper, measuring a mere 80 x 146mm, came from the workshop of William Caxton, who brought printing to England in 1476. It bears no date but the type used suggests a date of 1479. Its purpose was to bring to the public's notice the publication by Caxton of a pye 'of two and thre comemoracio[n]s of salisburi use'. This was a set of rules for special services to commemorate the saints according to the use established at Salisbury. It is historically important, however, on at least five grounds: it is the earliest printed advertisement in English; in announcing that it uses the same type as the book which it advertises ('enpryntid after the forme of this prese[n]t lettre whiche ben wel and truly correct')

it is the first English type specimen; it reveals Caxton's trade sign as the red pale ('at the reed pale'); and the Latin formula at its foot, which translates as 'Please leave this little notice where it is', indicates that it was a poster – the first printed in England. It also appears to contain a printer's error: 'the almonesrye' (i.e. the almonry within the Westminster Abbey precincts where the workshop was) should probably have read 'almosnerye'.

This very significant small slip of paper came to the library in 1834 in the bequest of Francis Douce. He also owned the only other copy known to exist, which is now in the John Rylands Library of Manchester University.

Arch. G e.37

If it plese ony man spirituel or temporel to bye ony
pyes of two and thre comemoraciõs of salisburi vse
enpryntid after the forme of this preset lettre whiche
ben wel and truly correct, late hym come to westmo-
nester in to the almonesrye at the reed pale and he shal
haue them good chepe ...

Supplico stet cedula

A camouflaged book

During the years of the Revolution in France at the end of the eighteenth century, church service books were systematically destroyed. This copy of the first edition of the missal for the use of Paris – the two-volume *Missale Parisiense*, printed on parchment in 1481 by Jean Du Pré and Desiderius Huym – is thus very rare; indeed, it is one of only four copies known to have survived. At the time of the purge it was over three hundred years old and a prized possession of those who took it under their protection, hiding its nature and antiquity by camouflaging its exterior to look like a revolutionary constitutional text.

The silver furniture was removed from its crimson velvet binding, where its outline and nail-holes may still be seen, and 'CONSTITUTION L'AN 3' inscribed on the front cover of Volume I. In the same way, 'Droits de l'homme' was written on the front cover of Volume II,

while on its last leaf (should anyone check further) the final article, no. 377, of the *Constitution de 5 Fructidor An. III* (22 August 1795) was copied out.

The first volume is open at the service for Christmas Day, the illuminated letter P beginning the phrase 'Puer natus est nobis' ('Unto us a child is born').

The missal was bought by the Bodleian Library for 10 guineas in 1842.

Auct. 6Q 3.24 cover and a9v – a10r; Auct. 6Q 3.25 cover and lower end leaf

Le Peuple français remet le dépôt de la présente
constitution à la fidélité du corps législatif, au
directoire exécutif, aux administrateurs et aux
juges; à la vigilance des pères de famille, aux
épouses et aux mères, à l'affection des jeunes
citoyens, au courage de tous les français.

[Left column 1]

Lux fulgebit hodie sup nos quia nat' e nobis dominus et vocabitur admirabilis deus princeps pacis pater futuri seculi cuius regni nõ erit finis. ps. Dñs regnauit decoē idutus e: idut' est dominus fortitudinē et precinxit se. Gloria patri filio. kyrieel. Gloria in excelsis deo. Orõ.

Da nobis quesum' omnipotēs de' vt qui noua incarnati verbi tui luce perfundimur: hoc in nro resplendeat opere. qd pfide fulget in mēte. Iste due oōnes dicuntur ad vnum per domiñ. De sancta anastasia.

Oratio. Da quesum' omnipotens de'. vt qui beate anastasie martyris tue solennia colimus eius apud te patrocinia sentiamus.

Lectio isaye ppheta lxi. Et dicit dominus de'. Spiritus domini sup me. eo qd vnxit me ad annunciandum mansuetis misit me. Vt medeter cõtritos corde. et predicarem captiuis indulgentiā: et clausis a prisone. Vt predicarē añu placabilē domino: et die vltiõis deo nostro vt consolarer ois lugētes et ponerē fortitudinē lugentibus syon. Et darem eis coronā pro cinere: oleū gaudij p luctu. palliū laudis pro spiritu meroris. et vocabuntur in ea fortes iustitie plātatio domini. ad glorificandum. Ecce dominus auditū fecit: icĩ.

[Left column 2]

tremis terre. Dicite filie syon: Ecce saluator tuus venit: ecce merces ei' cũ eo: et op' illius corã ipo. Et vocabit eos populus sanctus. redēpti a dõno deo nostro. Ad vñ.

Tertio caplo. Carissime. Apparuit benignitas et humanitas: saluatoris dei nostri. Nõ ex operib' iusticie que fecimus nos: sed secundū suã misericordiã. saluos nos fecit. Per lauacrũ regenerationis et renouationis spiritus sancti: que effudit i nos abunde. per iesum xpm saluatorē nostrum. vt iustificati gratia ipsius heredes simus secdm spē vite eterne. In christo iesu domino nostro. Ṝ. Benedictus qui venit in nomine dñi deus dñs et illuxit nobis. v. A domino factum est et est mirabile in oculis nostris. Ṝ. Alla Dominus regnauit decorē in tuit idut dñs fortitudinē et precinxit se virtute. Psla. Regnauit sempiterna. Querē ibi es seco aduentus. Secdm lucã.

In illo tempore. Pastores loquebantur adinuicem. Trãseamus vsq; bethlē: et videam' hoc verbū qd factũ est: qd dñs ostēdit nobis. Et venerũt festinātes: et inuenerūt mariã et ioseph et infantem positũ i presepio. Videntes autē eũ cognouerũt de verbo qd dictũ erat illis de puero hoc. Et omēs qui audierũt mirati sũt et de his que dicta erant a pastorib' ad ipsos. Maria aũt seruabat oīa verba hec: cõferens in corde suo. Et reuersi sunt pastores glorificantes et laudantes deum i omnib' que audierãt.

[Right column 1]

et viderant: sicut dictum est ad illos. Credo. Offtz. Deus enim firmauit ozbem terre qui non cõmouebit. parata sedes tua deus extunc a seculo tu es. Secreta.

Munera nostra quesum' domine natiuitatis hodierne mysteriis apta proueniant: vt sicut homo genitus idem refulsit deus: sic nobis hec terrena substātia conferat quod diuinum est. De sancta anastasia.

Accipe quesum' domie munera dignãter oblata: et beate anastasie suffragantibus meritis ad nostre salutis auxiliũ pueñire concede. Per dñm. Prefacio. Quia per incarnati. Et cõmunicantes. vt supra. Cõo. Exulta filia syon lauda filia hierusalē ecce rex tuo venit sctūs et saluator mūdi. postcõ.

Da nobis dñe sacramēti seper nouitas natalis instauret: cuiꝰ natiuitas singularis humanam reppulit vetustatem. De sancta anastasia. postcõ

Saciasti dñe familiã tuã muneribus sacris. eius qꝰ semper interuentione nos refoue: cuiꝰ solennia celebramus. Per dñm.

Ad magnam missam. Introitus. Puer natus est nobis. et filiꝰ datus est nobis cuius imperium super humerum ei'. et vocabit nomen ei' magni consilii angelus. ps. Cantate domino canticum nouũ quia mirabilia

[Right column 2]

fecit. Glia patri. Sicut. kyriel. Gloria in excelsis. Orõ.

Cõcede quesumus omnipotens deus: vt nos vnigeniti tui noua per carnē natiuitas liberet. quos sub peccati iugo vetusta seruitus tenet. Qui tecũ. Memonulla. Lectio isaye ppheta. lii.

Hec dicit dominus deus. Propter hoc sciet populus meꝰ nomē meũ i die illa: quia ego ipse qui loquebar ecce adsum. Quam pulchri super mõtes pedes annũciantis et predicantis pacem: annunciantis bonum. predicantis salutem: dicentis syon. regnabit deus tuus. Vox speculatorũ tuorum leuauerunt vocē: simul laudabunt quia oculo ad oculum videbunt.cũ conuerterit dñs syon. Gaudete et laudate simul deserta hierusalem: quia cõsolatus est dominus populũ suũ. et redemit hierusalem. Parauit dñs brachiũ sanctum suum: in oculis oim gētium. Et videbunt omēs fines terre salutare dei nostri. Lectio epistole bi pauli apli Ad hebreos. i. ca.

Fratres. Multiphariē multisqꝫ modis olim deus loquēs patribꝰ in prophis. nouissie diebꝫ istis locutus est nobis i filio: quē constituit heredem vniuersorum per quem fecit et secula. Qui cum sit splendor glorie et figura substātie eius. portansqꝫ omnia verbo virtutis sue purgationem pctõrum faciens: sedet ad dexterã maiestatis in excelsis. Tāto melior ãgelis effectꝰ: quāto differenti' pre illis nomē hereditauit. Cui ei dixit aliqñ

The earliest printed tourist guide

Bernhard von Breydenbach (1440–1497) was a wealthy canon of Mainz and, from 1484, dean of the cathedral there. In 1483, to ensure the salvation of his soul, he determined on a pilgrimage to the Holy Land, setting out from Venice on 1 June. In the party accompanying him was Erhard Reuwich, an artist from Utrecht who made sketches of places visited en route. Following their return to Venice in January 1484, Reuwich set about printing his drawings alongside an account of the tour credited to Breydenbach but probably compiled by Martin Roth, a Dominican from Pforzheim who was not himself one of the pilgrims. The resulting volume, Bernhard von Breydenbach, *Peregrinatio in terram sanctam* (Mainz: Erhard Reuwich, 11 Feb. 1486), can lay claim to being the earliest printed tourist guide.

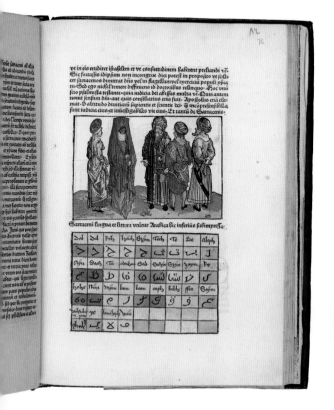

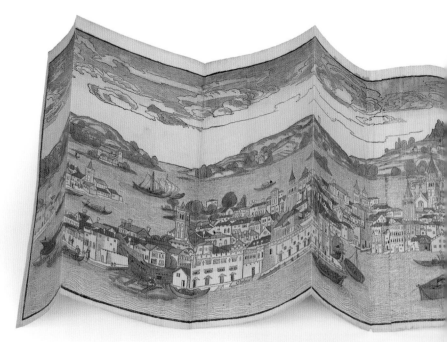

Reuwich's six panoramic views of cities and islands visited fold out from the volume, and this, too, is an innovation in print. That of Venice, shown here, is 1.5m in length, while that of the Holy Land with Jerusalem at its centre is larger still. The text is interspersed with further woodcut illustrations, some showing styles of dress worn by the inhabitants of regions through which the pilgrims passed and the pronunciation of the native languages. That shown here concerns Saracens.

The volume contains a wealth of other information, ranging from the histories of various sieges, recipes for remedies for seasickness, descriptions (and drawings) of animals encountered including a 'coppin' or baboon seen in the Holy Land, details of churches visited with notes on holy relics presented in them (the left arm and hand of St Katherine at Rhodes, for example,

and in Venice one of the six jars in which water was miraculously turned into wine at the wedding at Cana) and a description of an eclipse of the moon seen in October 1483 when the party was in Egypt visiting the Pyramids. The book may be seen as a fifteenth-century bestseller and it ran to twelve editions between this one in 1486 and 1522.

This copy belonged in the eighteenth century to Pietro-Antonio Bolognaro-Crevenna (1735–1792), an Italian snuff-trader in Amsterdam – most of whose great library was dispersed in a sale in 1790. The Bodleian Library bought many books at that sale, but not this one. It was bought by Francis Douce and came to the Bodleian with his collection in 1834.

Arch. B c.25, fol. 76 and map of Venice

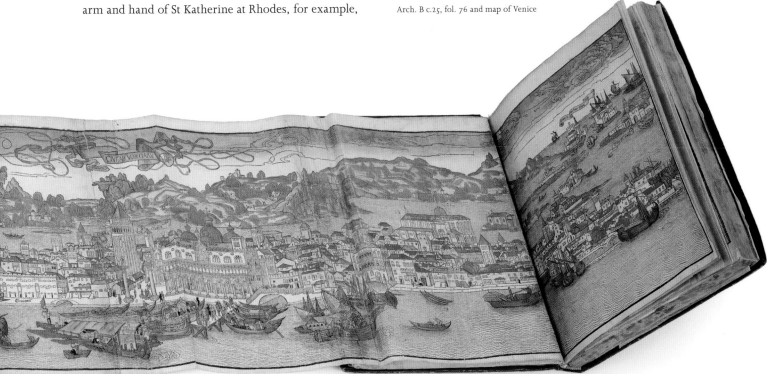

A pilgrimage of Persian birds

From its earliest days the Bodleian Library sought to acquire manuscripts from the east. Six years after it opened, in 1608, Sir Thomas Bodley asked Paul Pindar, consul of the English merchants in Aleppo, to collect for him 'bookes in the Syriacke, Arabicke, Turkishe and Persian tongues, or in any other language of those Eastern nations, bycause I make no doubt but in processe of time, by the extraordinairie diligence of some one or other student they may be readily understoode'. By the nineteenth century books and manuscripts in all these languages were among the library's strengths, and in 1859 the Bengal civil servant J.B. Elliott enriched its collections further with more than four hundred Arabic and Persian manuscripts, including that from which this illustration comes.

It decorates a copy made in 1493 of a poem in masnavi form, *Mantiq al-Tayr* or *Conference of the Birds* by the greatest Persian Sufi poet of the twelfth century, Shaykh Farid al-Din 'Attar Nishapuri (c.1145–c.1221). It is a tale concerning the quest for spiritual fulfilment. A gathering of birds listen to the hoopoe in the centre of the group as it tells them of the Simurgh (the divine being) – represented by the artist as a huge elaborately adorned bird – and how they should set out on a journey to seek it. Many decline to go while others set out but fall by the wayside. After a long journey only thirty arrive at the final destination, the home of the Simurgh. There the thirty birds (*si-murgh* in Persian) – realize that they have found spiritual fulfilment in themselves. The story of a long and arduous journey in search of spiritual enlightenment has parallels in many other literary traditions.

MS. Elliott 246, fol. 25v

The earliest English gold-tooled binding

In or about the year 1519 the schoolmaster and grammarian Robert Whittington (c.1480–1553) presented this book to Thomas Wolsey, by then archbishop of York, lord chancellor and a cardinal. It is a manuscript principally containing two works by Whittington: one in verse in praise of Wolsey dispensing justice in public administration, and the other in prose on the four cardinal virtues, dedicated to Wolsey. It was a blatant attempt to gain Wolsey's patronage. The book's contents are of no lasting importance, but its clothing is of outstanding significance.

Both the upper and lower cover carry the earliest known example of gold-tooled binding in England. The tooling was done not with heated irons but with wooden blocks pressed into the leather. The blocks were then removed. Gold was applied with glair to the indentations and the blocks replaced and held in a press for some hours. These blocks, clearly too large for a book this size and therefore placed sideways, represent St George slaying the dragon and (twice on the upper cover and once on the lower) three Tudor emblems: the rose, the portcullis and the pomegranate.

It was an impressive gift (gold-tooling did not become common for another thirty years), and apparently achieved its aim. Whittington was patronized by both Wolsey and Henry VIII. The book came to the Bodleian from an unknown source at some time in the years 1603–05.

MS. Bodl. 523, upper cover

110

Tudor calligraphy

This extraordinarily elaborate example of Tudor penmanship is the start of a working document. It is a long roll made up of twelve parchment skins glued end to end, the whole measuring 47cm wide and 828cm long. Written in a fine secretary hand, it records a survey made by Richard Pollard and Thomas Moyle in 1539 of 'all the Lordeships Manno[r]s landes tenements woodes parkes fysshing waters and other hereditamentes belonging to the late attainted Monasterie of Glastonburye lying and beyng in sondry Counties hereafter specified now in the kyngs handes by the attaincture of Richard Whiting late Abbat of the same of haute treason attainted'.

The Benedictine abbey at Glastonbury, prior to its dissolution, had the highest net income of any English monastery. Its property was a major acquisition for Henry VIII, and the somewhat insubstantial charges brought against Abbot Whiting did not save him from being dragged through the town's streets on a hurdle and then hanged, drawn and quartered on Glastonbury Tor.

The two initial letters T which begin the word 'The' in the heading and in the document's first line are extremely accomplished. The first encloses musicians, three dancing putti, a pair of wrestlers whose lower limbs merge with the foliage and a musical owl and ape. It flows into the royal arms with, above it, 'VIVAT REX' repeated three times, on a ribbon above Tudor roses. The second encloses a figure whose ribbon reads 'Veritas tandem vincet' and flows across the ascenders of two letters 'h' into a drawing of a turbaned figure labelled Solymon Turkischer (i.e. Suleiman I the Magnificent, sultan of the Ottoman Empire when this document was compiled). It was given to the Bodleian in 1751 by the antiquary and MP Charles Gray.

MS. Bodl. Rolls 19

Elizabeth I's books

Queen Elizabeth I much preferred embroidered or velvet bindings to leather ones on her shelves. She demonstrated this preference early in life when aged 11. As a New Year's gift for her stepmother Queen Katherine Parr in 1544/5, she translated and then wrote out a French devotional poem 'Le miroir de l'âme pécheresse' ('The mirror or glass of a sinful soul') by Margaret of Angoulême, heading it with the words: 'To our moste noble and vertuous quene Katherin, Elizabeth her humble daughter wisheth perpetuall felicitie and everlasting joye'. The parchment leaves on which she wrote were then clad in a binding, possibly embroidered by the princess herself, with silver and gold stitches on a blue silk ground and with the queen's initials in the centre.

Almost forty years later in 1584, when she was herself queen, Elizabeth received a beautifully bound book as a New Year's present – from the royal printer Christopher Barker. It was a Bible printed by Barker in 1583 'covered wt crimson vellat alover embradered wythe venys golde and seade perle', and it has been truly described as 'the most decorative and in many ways the finest of all remaining embroidered books of the time'. The floral decoration features Tudor roses executed in silver and gold thread and coloured silks on a crimson velvet background. A silk bookmarker is similarly decorated.

It is not known how either of these books escaped from the Royal Collection. The princess's gift came to the Bodleian in 1729 from the widow of Francis Cherry, a wealthy Berkshire landowner. The Bible was part of the great collection of manuscripts and books bequeathed by Francis Douce in 1834.

MS. Cherry 36, binding; Douce Bib.Eng. 1583, b.1, binding

Aztec pictographs

The Bodleian possesses a number of early items from the period before, and the half-century following, Columbus's voyage to the New World. They include four Mexican manuscripts of pre-Columbian style, a strip taken from the battle standard of Francisco Pizarro in his campaigns against the Inca Empire in the 1530s (given to the British secretary of state for foreign affairs in 1856) and, perhaps the most remarkable of all, the Codex Mendoza. This is an Aztec pictographic manuscript prepared on the orders of Don Antonio de Mendoza (1491–1552), the first viceroy of new Spain, shortly after the conquest of Mexico. Its purpose was to inform and enlighten the Council of the Indies at Seville and, more particularly, the Emperor Charles V, about the history and customs of the inhabitants of this new addition to his empire.

It is a book in three parts written by a Mexican painter of books. The glyphs or pictographs which he produced were interpreted verbally to a Spanish priest who spoke the Nahuatl language. The priest then annotated the drawings in Spanish and provided an introduction and notes. The codex's seventy-one leaves contain, first, a copy of a lost chronicle which tells the story of the gradual domination of the country by the Aztec lords of Tenochtitlan from 1325 until the fall of the empire in 1521; second, a copy of the roll showing the tribute due yearly from some four hundred towns to the last emperor, Moctezuma II; and, third, composed by the artist himself especially for the viceroy, an account of Aztec life 'from year to year'.

The leaves reproduced here are from this last section and show the treatment of children between the ages of 3 and 14 (as indicated by the blue dots). Boys, taught by their fathers, are shown on the left, and girls, taught by their mothers, on the right. Alongside each is an indication of their mealtime rations: half, one, one and a half, or two tortillas as their ages increase. Between the ages of 3 and 6 girls learn the names of items in the workbasket and how to use a spindle; the boys carry light loads, fetch water, are sent to the market to collect scraps and learn how to use a fishing net. Between 8 and 10 they may become disobedient and are punished with beatings and with being stuck with maguey (agave) spikes. At 11 and 12, the punishments get worse: the boy is forced to inhale smoke from burning capsicums, bound hand and foot and laid out on damp ground; the girl is woken up at night and sent out to sweep the streets. As teenagers, things improve: the boy cuts reeds and goes fishing, the girl cooks and weaves.

Since this unique and supremely important document for the interpretation of Aztec languages and custom was intended for Charles V, one might wonder why it is in the Bodleian Library and has been there since 1659.

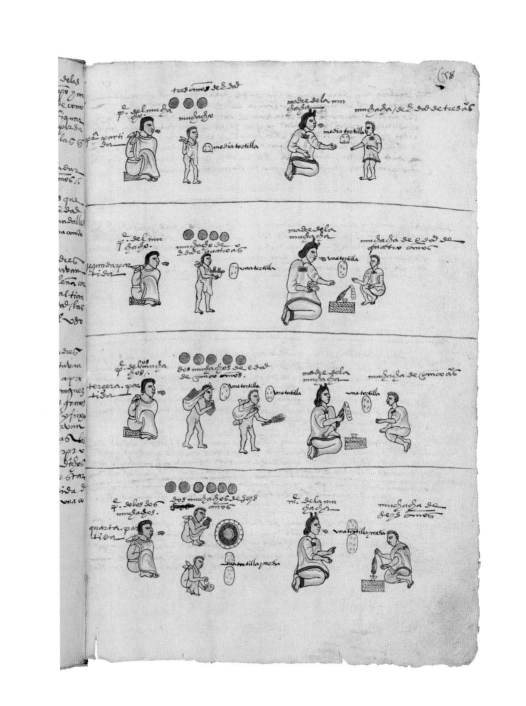

tres oños de edad

p̃. del me dia
mudado

media tortilla

madre de la mu
dada

mudada / se edad de tres añs

p̃ partidor

p̃. del mu
dado.

mudado de
edad de quatro añs

una tortilla

madre de la
mudada

mudada de edad de
quatro oños

segunda par
tida

p̃. del mucha
chos.

dos muchados de esa
de çinco oños

madre de la
mudada

muchacha de çinco añs

tercera par
tida

una tortilla

una tortilla

p̃. delos dos
mudados.

dos muchados de seis
oños

m̃. dela mu
chada

muchacha de
seys oños

quarta par
tida

una tortilla y media

una tortilla y media

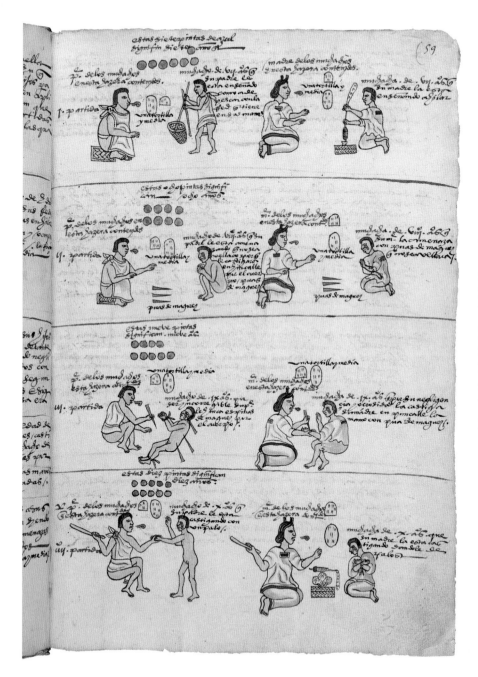

The answer lies in the fact that it never reached Spain. It was completed in a hurry, the Spanish priest having been delayed by arguments among his native informants about the meaning of some of the glyphs. Nevertheless, it reached Hispaniola (Santo Domingo) in time to catch the fleet before it set sail for the Iberian peninsula. En route, however, the ship carrying it was captured by a French man-of-war and the codex is next documented as being owned by André Thevet, geographer to Henri II of France. Thevet dated his

acquisition 1553, and some thirty years later sold it to the English geographer Richard Hakluyt. On Hakluyt's death in 1616, it was inherited by Samuel Purchas, the travel writer and compiler of *Pilgrimes*, who regarded it as 'the choicest of my jewels'. After he died it passed into the hands of the lawyer and book-collector John Selden (d. 1654), and came to the Bodleian Library with most of his vast collection of manuscripts and books.

MS. Arch. Selden. A. 1, fols 58r, 59r, 60r

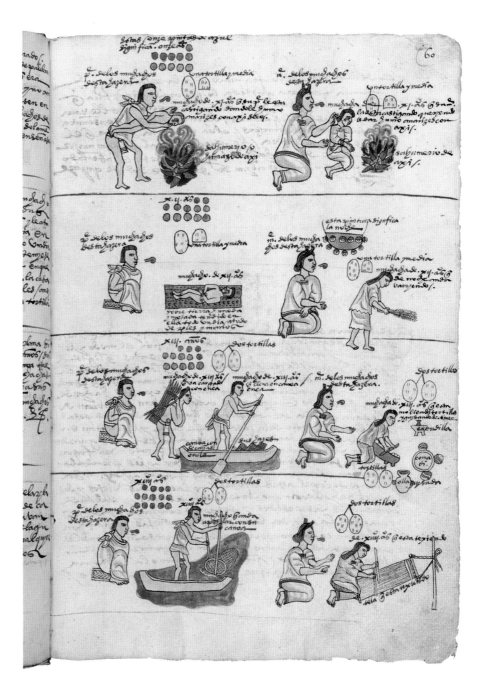

Tipu Sultan's Qur'an

Tipu Sultan (1750–1799), known as the Tiger of Mysore, was the eldest son of Haider Ali, and succeeded him as the last ruler of the southern Indian kingdom of Mysore in 1782. A permanent thorn in the flesh of British rule in India, he died at the Battle of Seringapatam in the fourth Anglo–Mysore War in 1790. After his death his library of some two thousand books was seized by the British East India Company and from it two very fine copies of the Qur'an were presented by the Court of Directors, one to the Bodleian Library and one to Cambridge University Library in 1806.

The Bodleian copy is illustrated here. It was written in 1550 on 344 leaves of glazed paper measuring 39 x 25cm, probably in Shiraz in Iran by 'Alā' al-Din Muhammad ibn al-Mahmūd al-Saljūqi, whose signature appears at the end of the book, and it is a fine example of the book art that flourished during the era of the Persian Safarid dynasty (1501–1722). The beautifully intricate illuminated opening (fols 9v –10r) is typical of the period: the two central medallions containing the opening chapter of the Qur'an are written in white in the Naskhī script widely used for copying the holy book. Its contemporary morocco binding is elaborately stamped inside and out and coloured principally with gold, blue, green, red and white.

MS. Bodl. Or. 793 binding and fols 9v–10r

A Greek bestiary in France

This group of depictions of animals comes from a manuscript in Greek written and painted in France in 1564. The text is that of a bestiary originally compiled by Manuel Philes, who lived from 1275 to c.1340, and this copy is one of several made and signed by Angelos Vergikios, who had come to France in 1538 from his native Crete via Venice and worked there as a much admired scribe for the next thirty years until his death in 1569. Written on sixty-three leaves of paper, it includes 111 illustrations, and tradition has it that these were executed by Angelos Vergikios's daughter. Her name, however, is unknown and apart from this tradition there is little, if any, evidence even of her existence.

Whoever the artist was, the pictures are very appealing and remarkably lifelike. The first section of the work is concerned with animals that fly, and includes the heron, cockerel and owl. The second section, which includes the elephant, the fox, and the rabbit is of four-legged beasts, insects and snakes. The last section covers aquatic beasts.

The manuscript – together with another written by the same scribe – was a gift to Sir Thomas Bodley in 1601 prior to the Library's opening from his friend Sir John Fortescue (1533–1607), a loyal servant of the Crown.

MS. Auct. F. 4. 15, details from fols. 60v (crabs), 5v (heron), 33r (fox), 27r (elephant), 11r (cockerel)

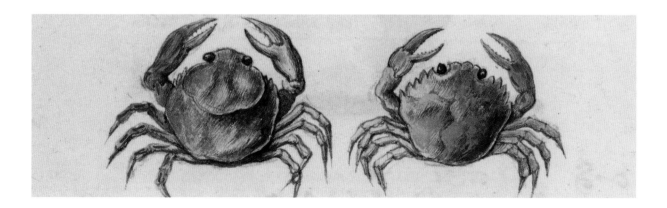

ἐρωδιός.

ἀλώπηξ

ἐλέφας

ἀλεκτρυών

An illustrated Arabic encyclopedia

Among the remarkable Arabic items that Archbishop William Laud's agents brought back to him from the east, and which he subsequently gave to the Bodleian Library in 1639, is this illustrated copy, made in 1560, of the *Rasà'il Ikhwān al-Safā* or the Epistles of the Brethren of Sincerity.

The Brethren of Sincerity or Brethren of Purity were a group believed to have been active in Basra in the tenth century, and the fifty-two epistles form a kind of encyclopedia covering a great range of mathematical, scientific, philosophical and theological subjects, claiming to be a 'complete account of all things' set down for the 'refinement of the soul and the improvement of morals'.

In this sixteenth-century copy made some seventy years before Laud acquired it, the epistles on animals are particularly well illustrated. The folios shown here accompany sections explaining the reasons for the existence of animals such as the elephant and the camel, with comments on their physical characteristics. Written on paper, the book consists of 367 leaves measuring 31 x 20cm within a fine contemporary eastern leather binding with gold-stamped inlaid central medallions and corner pieces.

MS. Laud Or.260, fols 123v–124r and binding

للادب فرزان لمل بكر دنارا لدوطا وعطبا ثالثار والعبب

الخادمسوب الدت دطل عذا النار يدكاجيوان جمله قالبه ثل الاعضا
ونادرن طرولير الجل موضع غر الرعه ودراه سدليدت نطاى الروطاته راه زلما
عه دنع ايدا لا مدم شنبب لخروج ايباه بنده وابناء سلاح له دفع انساى
غلاظام بلوله داطلام ثل اعطى ظول طوظه ثالرى دابا الذى قرت الى لا بصى
برطر لمون دناهى برعرف بيه عذا ناثر الجد صراف ونت ثل مبدنانا ارباب

The story of Yusuf and Zulaykha

This sixteenth-century Persian manuscript is one of fifty-five books purchased in 1678 by the Bodleian Library from the estate of Thomas Greaves DD, a theologian who deputized for the first Laudian professor of Arabic at Oxford when he was abroad and who died in 1676. He had inherited them from his brother John, a noted orientalist and astronomer, in 1652.

Written and illustrated in 1569, it contains the text of one of the great poetic mystical love stories of Islamic literature, *Yusuf u Zulaykha*, written in 1484 by the scholar and theologian 'Abd al-Rahman Jami (d. 1494). The story of Yusuf or Joseph is one common to many different traditions. In its Christian biblical version recorded in Genesis, Joseph, sold into slavery in Egypt by his brothers, is imprisoned after resisting the blandishments of his master Potiphar's wife, but is eventually released and rises to become governor of Egypt and to forgive his brothers. In Jami's epic version the prophet Yusuf, sold into slavery, resists the advances of Zulaykha and is imprisoned. On his release he prospers and after many years meets Zulaykha again and they marry. Zulaykha's profane love is transformed into divine and lasting love. The illustration opposite depicts Yusuf as a slave serving Zulaykha while her female servants are overcome by his beauty. The whole manuscript is clothed in a contemporary binding of dark green lacquer painted with depictions of animals, birds, trees and flowers; the doublure is of decorated leather.

MS. Greaves 1, fols. 103v–104r

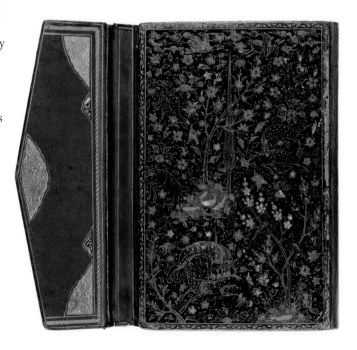

126

The Persian text on the right page:

بدانش که دیدن عالمک دوست — نخست از جان روشن بین دست دوست
نیارم بعد ازین کنفج جویم روی — کز مرد صفت کنامم پیشم روی
زعشقش تخت آن زین سخت گفت — برون آمد بگوش بکلفزار نشست
زمان مصر کمال گلزار دیدند — یکی پیکار زروشتان ننت
بزی پاکل انش کمال یارچد ند — عنان بتاب ای یزدتان ننت
جوسیک روزان پارین — زحرت جون تریخ جهان عالمند
دانسته تریخ ازدست خود یافا — تنش تریخ خود بریدین
کمی تریخ ننشسته حکم کرد — زدت خود برید بک وفانی
اقلم هرکه باتیمی نبستردند — زمر بندش وهشکوف ینزد — بدل صفت وفانی نفشم کرد

Akbar I's album

The Mughal emperors from central Asia held sway in India from the sixteenth to the eighteenth centuries, and during their rule a vigorous painting culture developed, absorbing influences from both the east and the west. The Bodleian acquired its first Mughal paintings in an album presented by Archbishop Laud in 1640. The one illustrated here arrived as part of the great legacy of Francis Douce in 1834.

Akbar, who ruled from 1556 to 1605, was the grandson of Babur, the founder of the dynasty. Unable to read or write himself, he was nevertheless a great patron of the arts. Under him painting, architecture and a variety of religious traditions flourished. Akbar was fascinated by Christian subjects seen in engravings reaching the court from traders and Jesuit missionaries in Goa. This painting of St Matthew was executed in 1588 by one of Akbar's leading artists, Kesu Das, and derives from an engraving after the Dutch painter Maerten van Heemskerck (1498–1574). The evangelist is shown writing 'sanctus Matheus Evangelista' in a volume held by his symbol, the angel, who also holds his inkpot. The angel's knee, supporting the book, rests on St Matthew's thigh. They are shown in front of a pavilion by the side of an Indian lotus lake with a European town in the hills beyond. A cat and decorative pots embellish the foreground. The blue ewer bears the artist's name and date.

MS. Douce Or. a. 1, fol. 41v

A topographical tapestry

In the 1590s Ralph Sheldon (1537–1613) commissioned four tapestry maps to be woven to decorate his new house at Weston in Warwickshire. Each map covered a county where the Sheldon family lived or had friends and relations, or had landholdings built up by astute marriages and shrewd purchases following the dissolution of the monasteries. The counties were Oxfordshire, Warwickshire, Worcestershire and Gloucestershire. Because of the way weaving was done a tapestry had to be quadrilateral. County boundaries, however, are not and so each map contained more than its individual county. Thus, when they were, presumably, hung on the walls of his new house, Ralph Sheldon was presented not with a navigational aid but with an artistic panoramic view across England from Bristol to London.

The Sheldon family was a Catholic one. Their properties were pillaged during the Civil War and over the years these remarkable maps suffered some damage and escaped into other hands. Two of them were replaced later in the seventeenth century by new ones made by weavers commissioned by Sheldon's great-grandson. Of the original four, two (Oxfordshire and Worcestershire) were bequeathed to the Bodleian Library by the antiquary Richard Gough in 1809, though part of Oxfordshire had been cut off and made into a fire-screen which is now in the Victoria and Albert Museum. The Warwickshire map is now in that county's museum collection. The fourth, Gloucestershire, remained in private hands until 2007 when it appeared on the market. The Bodleian Library, aided by its Friends organisation, the Art Fund and a variety of trusts and foundations, bought it for a sum in excess of £100,000.

Created within two decades of Christopher Saxton's first mapping of the country, county by county, these are remarkable examples of the art of Elizabethan tapestry weavers. Shown here is that part of one of the maps depicting the area to the west of Oxford.

LONGE·COMB
KIDLINGTON
ISLIPP
BLADON
BAGBROKE
WATEREATON
YARNTON
LONGE
HANBORO
CASSENTON
WOLVERCOT
MARSTON
HEDDENDON
S·LEE
AYNSHAM
OXFORD
WITHAM
BOTLEY
ISELEY
STAVNTON
HAVTINCOVRT
HINKSEY
CVMNOR
KENNINGTON
SANFORD
N·MORE
STANLAKE

William Shakespeare

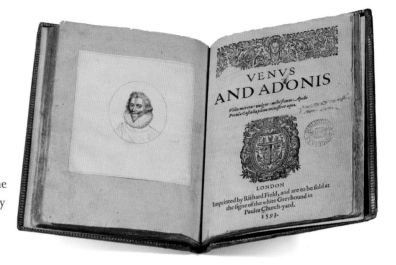

The copy (right) of *Venus and Adonis*, the first of Shakespeare's works to be published – in 1593 – and the only copy known to exist, came to the Bodleian Library as part of the collection made by the Shakespearian editor Edmund Malone in 1821. Had it been offered to Sir Thomas Bodley as a recently published poem when he was acquiring books for his new library while Shakespeare was at his most productive, he would probably have rejected it as not fit for the sort of scholarly collection at which he aimed. In the library's early years its involvement with Shakespearian items was not particularly fortunate. Its agreement with the Stationers' Company, for instance, resulted in the arrival into the library as a new book a copy of what is now perhaps the most celebrated of all English literary productions: the First Folio of Shakespeare's *Works*. That copy, illustrated here, arrived in sheets and was sent to a local man, William Wildgoose, to be bound before being chained and placed on the shelves. The record of its despatch to Wildgoose survives. However, when the Third Folio was received in 1664 and was thought of as a better and more complete edition, the First Folio was eliminated from the library. By great good fortune it survived in private hands and when in 1905 it was brought into the library for advice, its binding was soon recognized as by Wildgoose and its identity as the Bodleian original established. Following a public subscription it was reacquired by the library in 1906.

Over the centuries the Bodleian's collections have enabled the University of Oxford to become one of the great centres for the study of sixteenth- and seventeenth-century English literature. It is therefore fitting that alongside Shakespeare's earliest published verse the library should also hold the most complete copy of one of the latest additions to the canon of his poetic works. In 1986 a previously disregarded poem 'Shall I dye? Shall I flye?' in a pre-1640 manuscript commonplace book in the library was deemed by the editors of Oxford University Press's edition of *The Complete Oxford Shakespeare* (1987) to be by the playwright. The manuscript in which it survives, where its attribution to Shakespeare had always previously been discounted, came to the library in 1755 in the collection of Richard Rawlinson.

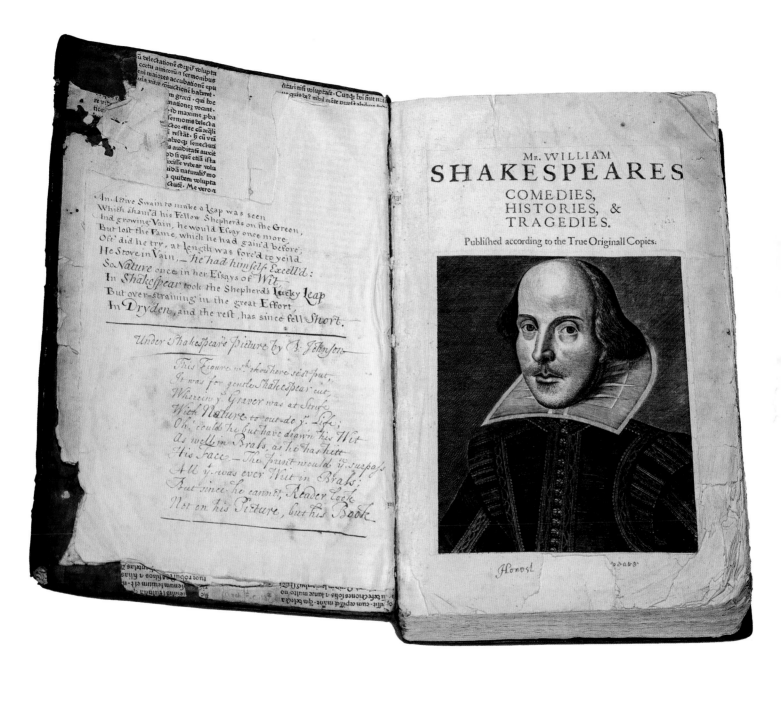

An Active Swain to make a Leap was seen
Which sham'd his Fellow Shepherds on the Green,
And growing Vain, he would Essay once more,
But lost the Fame, which he had gain'd before;
Oft' did he try, at length was forc'd to yeild
He Strove in Vain, — he had himself Excell'd:
So Nature once in her Essays of Wit
In Shakespear took the Shepherd's lucky Leap
But over-straining in the great Effort,
In Dryden, and the rest, has since fell Short.

Under Shakespeare's Picture by B. Johnson

This Figure which thou here seest put,
It was for gentle Shakespear cut;
Wherein ye Graver was at Strife
With Nature to out-do ye Life;
Oh, could he but have drawn his Wit
As well in Brass, as he has hitt
His Face — The print would ye surpass
All ye was ever Writ in Brass;
But since he cannot, Reader look
Not on his Picture, but his Book.

Mr. WILLIAM
SHAKESPEARES
COMEDIES,
HISTORIES, &
TRAGEDIES.

Published according to the True Originall Copies.

A SONNET

1

It is not long since I could see
And when the day did rise
I knew t'was light, but now from me
Tis hidden in yor eyes

2

Then, sweetest, since I only know
to Judge by your bright ray
Shine to your selfe for I will goe
I sweare none other way.

3

There I may see in yor sweet frame
heavens mold with all its blisse
Which though not mortall eye could name
Ile taste it in a kisse

4

Yet by noe power can I ere finde,
my sight if you not showe
Yo^r owne faire beames, Ile still be blinde
Unless sine cur'd by you,

A SONNET

1

Thou sentst to me a heart was sound,
I tooke it to be thine
But when I saw it had a wound,
I knew ye heart was myne,

2

A bounty of a strong conceipt
to send myne owne to me
And send it in a worse estate
Then when it came to thee.

3

The heart I sent thee had noe staine,
It was intire and sound,
But thou hast sent it backe againe
Sick of a deadly wound.

4

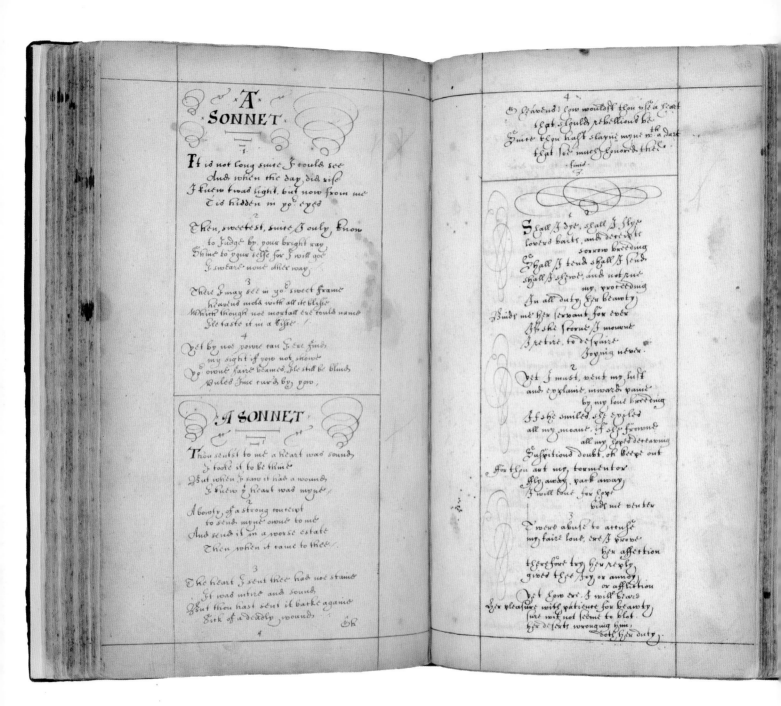

heavens how wouldst thou use a heart
that should rebellious be
Since thou hast slaine myne wth a dart
that soe much honor'd thee.
fins:

1

Shall I dye, shall I flye
loved harts, and desире
sorrow breeding
Shall I tend shall I send
shall I shewe, and not rue
my proceeding
In all duty, her beawty
Bids me her servant for ever
As she scorne I mournt
I retire, to despaire
Joyning never.

2

Yet I must, vent my lust
and explaine, inward paine
by my soule breeding
If she smiled, she exiled
all my moane, if she frownd
all my hopes deceaving
Suspicious doubt, oh keepe out
For thou art my, tormentor
Fly away, park away
I will love, for love
bids me venter

3

T'were abuse to accuse
my faire love, ere I prove
her assertion
therefore try her reply
gives thee Joy or annoy
or affliction
Yet how ere I will beard
her pleasure with patience for beawty
sure will not seeme to blot
her deserts wronging him
doth her duty.

In a dreame it did seeme
but alas, dreames doe passe
          as doe shaddowes
I did walke, I did talke
with my loue, with my doue
          through faire meadowes
Still wee past till at last
wee sate to repose us
          for o.r pleasure
being set lipp'd mett
armed freinds & did binde
          my hearts treasure
          5
Gentle winde sport did finde
wantonly to make fly,
          her gold tresses
As they shooke, I did looke
but her faire did impaire
          all my senses
As amaz'd, I gaz'd
On more then a mortall complextion
thee that loue, can proue
Such force in beauties inflextion
          6
Next her haire, fore head faire
smooth and high next doth lye
          without wrinkle
Her faire browes under those
star like eyes, win loued prize
          when they twinkle
In her cheekes, whose seekes
I shall finde there displayd beauties banner
oh admiring, desiring
breedes as I looke still vpon her
          7
Thin lipps red, fancies fed
with all sweets when he meets
          and is granted
There to trade, and is made
happy sure; to endure
          still vndaunted

pretty chinne, doth winne
Of all that's cal'd comendations
fairest necke, noe speck
All her parts meritt high admirations
          8
A pretty bare, past compare
parts those plotts (which besets)
          still asunder
It is meet, neught but sweet
should come neere, that soe rare
          is a wonder
Noe mishap, noe scape
Inferior to natures perfextion
noe blot, noe spot
Shee's beauties queene in electtion
          9
Whilst I dreamt, I exempt
for all care seem'd to share
          pleasures in plenty,
but awake care take
for I finde to my minde
          pleasures scanty
Therefore I will trie
to compasse my hearts cheife contenting
to delay, some saye
In such a case causeth repenting
          William Shakespeare

On my .d. & mistress
the Lady Elisabeth elected
Queene of Bohemia.

Yow violets, y.t doe first appeare
by richly purpled mantled knowne
Like those proud virgins of y.e yeare
As if the spring were all yo.r owne
          yow

A book no one in Oxford could read

Among the 'great store of honourable friends' on whom Sir Thomas Bodley relied to help him establish his library was Henry Percy, ninth earl of Northumberland, who was called the Wizard Earl because of his interest in science. In 1603 he gave Bodley £100 to spend on books. One of those acquired, inscribed by Bodley himself as a gift from the earl in 1604, was the Bodleian Library's first Chinese book. It was, in many ways, an extraordinary acquisition. No one in Oxford at that time could read Chinese. Further, Bodley's own inability to do so and his lack of understanding of the difference between the construction of an oriental book and that of a western one meant that his inscription is upside down at the back of the book. Presumably because of its impenetrability, it was not listed along with the other books bought with the earl's money in the Library's Benefactors' Register, nor did it appear in the printed catalogues of 1605 and 1620.

It was not catalogued until 1687, eighty-three years after its acquisition. Then it was identified as containing chapters 4–6 of the Analects of Confucius with the whole of Mencius, and is part of a cheap edition of the 'Four Books' (Si shu) of Confucius printed from blocks at Chien-yang in Fu-chien province during the Wanli period – the last quarter of the sixteenth century. These cheap productions of popular texts were regularly brought from south-east Asia by merchants of the Dutch East India Company and dispersed in Amsterdam. This was not the sort of book that scholarly libraries in China would have collected, and Sir Thomas Bodley (with his known antipathy to similar European productions, which he called 'baggage books') would almost certainly have rejected it had he known what it was.

Ironically books such as this one, because they were not collected, are now very rare. The survival of this copy illustrates and vindicates the founder's principle of acquiring materials as much for the future as for the present.

Sinica 2, fols. 1b–2a

136

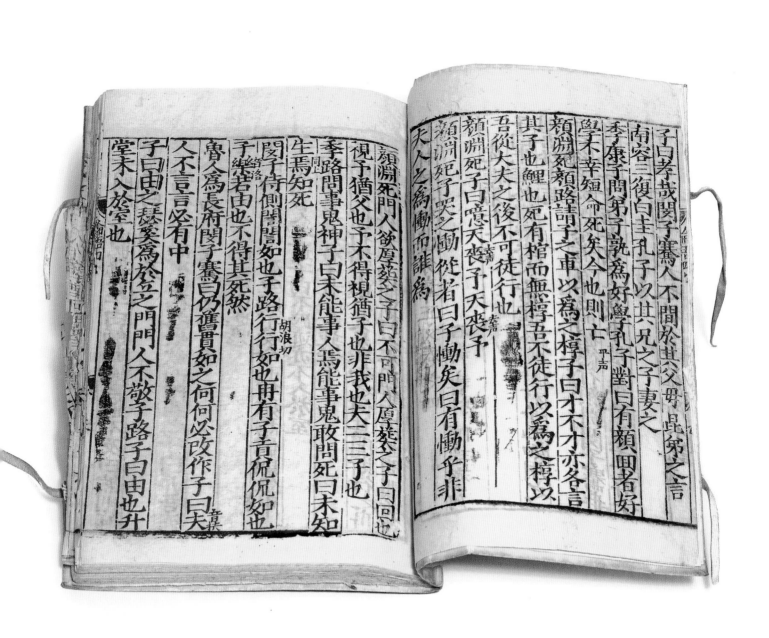

子曰孝哉閔子騫人不間於其父母昆弟之言

南容三復白圭孔子以其兄之子妻之

季康子問弟子孰爲好學孔子對曰有顏回者好

學不幸短命死矣今也則亡

顏淵死顏路請子之車以爲之椁子曰才不才亦各言

其子也鯉也死有棺而無椁吾不徒行以爲之椁以

吾從大夫之後不可徒行也

顏淵死子曰噫天喪予天喪予

顏淵死子哭之慟從者曰子慟矣曰有慟乎非

夫人之爲慟而誰爲

顏淵死門人欲厚葬之子曰不可門人厚葬之子曰回也

視予猶父也予不得視猶子也非我也夫二三子也

季路問事鬼神子曰未能事人焉能事鬼敢問死曰未知

生焉知死

閔子侍側誾誾如也子路行行如也冉有子貢侃侃如

子樂若由也不得其死然

魯人爲長府閔子騫曰仍舊貫如之何何必改作子曰夫

人不言言必有中

子曰由之瑟奚爲於丘之門門人不敬子路子曰由也升

堂未入於室也

Don Quixote

As well as gathering in manuscripts and books from the past for his newly opened library, Sir Thomas Bodley acquired new books. Among them were many in a format smaller than the shelves in the library (which were principally designed for folios) could sensibly accommodate, and some of which he might not wholly have approved. In particular, his letters to his first librarian make clear his dislike of the presence of works of fiction in a scholarly library.

The book illustrated here might have failed the test on both counts: it is a small book and a work of fiction. It is a copy of the first edition of Miguel de Cervantes Saavedra, *El ingenioso hidalgo de la Mancha, Don Quixote*, bought in Seville by the London bookseller John Bill, whom Bodley had employed to go to Spain in 1604 to purchase Spanish items. At a time of Anglo–Spanish tension Bill got no further than Seville but he did buy a quantity of books, the cost being covered by a gift of £100 from the earl of Southampton, Henry Wriothesley, the patron of Shakespeare and a supporter of Bodley's endeavours.

Don Quixote is a spoof of the sort of knightly romance then very popular throughout Europe and its presence on the Bodleian shelves is testimony to the reliance Bodley placed on the professional expertise of booksellers such as John Bill. It is now an extremely rare book. In the limp vellum binding which it still retains, it was placed on the new shelves built for smaller volumes in the gallery of Arts End. It remained there for almost four centuries until moved into an area of greater security in 1997.

Arch. B e.53

aunque defnudo de aquel preciofo ornamento de elegancia, y erudicion, de que fuelen andar veftidas las obras que fe componen en las cafas de los hombres que faben, ofe parecer fegura-mente en el juyzio de algunos, que continien-dofe en los limites de fu ignorancia, fuelen cõ-denar con mas rigor, y menos jufticia, los tra-bajos agenos, que poniendo los ojos la prudencia de vueftra Excelencia en mi buen deffeo, fio, que no defdeñarà la cortedad de tan humilde feruicio.

Miguel de Ceruantes Saauedra.

DESOCY-

PRIMERA PARTE
DEL INGENIOSO
hidalgo don Quixote de
la Mancha.

Capitulo Primero. Que trata de la condi-cion, y exercicio del famofo hidalgo don Quixote de la Mancha.

N Vn lugar de la Mancha, de cuyo nombre no quiero acor-darme, no ha mucho tiempo que viuia vn hidalgo de los de lança en aftillero, adarga anti-gua, rozin flaco, y galgo corre-dor. Vna olla de algo mas vaca que carnero, falpicon las mas noches, duelos y quebrátos los Sabados, lantejas los Viernes, algun palomino de aña-didura los Domingos: confumian las tres partes de fu hazienda. El refto della concluìan, fayo de velarte, calças de velludo para las fieftas, con fus pantuflos de

A   lo

A poem in John Donne's hand

No poem in English by John Donne (1572–1631) in his own handwriting was known to exist, until this single sheet was discovered in 1970 among the family papers of the duke of Manchester and was bought by the Bodleian Library. It remains the only one known to survive.

It is a verse addressed 'To the Honorable lady the lady Carew' and was published (from a copy) in 1633, in *Poems by J D* under the title 'A Letter to the Lady Carey, and Mrs Essex Riche, From Amyens'. The two women were sisters, Lettice Carey and Essex Rich, daughters of Sir Robert Rich, first earl of Warwick, and his second wife, Penelope Devereux (Philip Sidney's Stella). Their brother, Sir Robert Rich, was a friend of Donne who, on his way to Turin, met up with him in Amiens where Donne lived from December 1611 to March 1612. It was presumably at Rich's suggestion that Donne wrote this flattering verse epistle which Rich would then have sent to his sisters, recommending to their patronage the impoverished poet whom they had never met. The poem, written in tercets, praises the virtue of Lady Carey, who was the wife of Sir George Carey – flattery rendered ironic by subsequent rumours of her having borne an illegitimate daughter.

MS. Eng. poet. d. 197

140

Madame

Here where by all all Saints invoked are,
T'were too much scisme to bee singular,
And gainst a practise generall to warr;
Yett turninge to Saints, should my Humilitee
To other Saint then yow directed bee,
That were to make my scisme Heresee:
nor would I bee a Convertite so cold
As not to tell yow, If thys bee to bold,
Pardons are in thys market cheafly sold;
Where because fayth ys in too lowe degree,
I thought yt some Apostleship in mee
To speak things wch by fayth alone I see:
That ys, of yow, who are a firmament
Of vertues, where no one ys growen, nor spent,
Thay are yr Matercalls not yr Ornament.
Others, whom wee call vertuous, are not so
In theyr whole Substance but theyr vertues grow
But in theyr humors, and at Seasons show.
For when through tastles flatt Humilitee
In Doe-bak'd men some harmelesnes wee see,
Tis but hys flegme thats vertuous and not hee.
So ys the bloode sometymes, who euer ran
To danger vnimportun'd, hee was than
no better then a Sanguine vertuous man.
So Cloystrall Men who in pretence of feare,
All contributions to thys Lyfe forbear,
Haue vertu in Melancholy, and onely there.
Spirituall Cholerique Critiqs, wch in all
Religions fynd faults, and forgiue no fall
Haue through thys Zeale, vertu but in theyr Gall.
We are thus but parcell-gilt; To Gold we are growen,
When vertu ys our Soules Complexione.
who knowes hys vertues Name, or place, hath none.
Vertu ys but Aguishe when tis Seuerall;
By occasion wak'd, and Circumstantiall;
True vertu ys Soule, allways in all deeds all.
Thys vertu, thinkinge to giue Dignitee
To yr Soule found there no infirmitee;
for yr Soule was as good vertu as shee.
Shee therfore wrought upon that part of yow
wch ys scarce lesse then Soule as shee could doe,
And soe hath made yr Beauty vertue too;

The first Englishman in Japan

In 1598 William Adams, a seafarer and navigator from Gillingham in Kent, signed on as pilot of a Dutch ship sailing west across the Atlantic. The ship eventually reached the Pacific by way of the Strait of Magellan and then sailed on a perilous journey until it reached Japan in April 1600. Adams became the first Englishman recorded as having set foot in that country. At that time Japan was very hostile to foreigners and particularly to traders from western Europe. Adams, however, prospered and was befriended by Ieyasu Tokugawa, the shogun who had assumed power in 1600 and founded a dynasty that lasted until 1867. The shogun granted Adams a small estate on the Miura peninsula, and there he stayed until his death in 1620 – having remarried despite already having a wife and children in England. In Japan, where his fame is far greater than in Britain, he is known as Miura Anjin (the Miura pilot).

The document illustrated here owes much to his influence with the shogun. Dated 12 October 1613 (the 28th day of the 8th month, the 18th year of the Keicho), it has been called the first trade agreement between Japan and England. It is a shuinjo (vermillion seal document), the seal being that of Ieyasu Tokugawa. It was given to John Saris, the commander of the English East India Company's eighth voyage. Two years earlier the Dutch had been granted a monopoly of trade with Japan, but this document granted the English company the right to trade throughout Japan in all goods without hindrance and exempt from customs and other duties.

The Bodleian Library acquired items relating to Japan early in its history. Indeed, in 1620 Sir Thomas Bodley's friend Sir Henry Savile gave the library one of William Adams's ship's logbooks, written in his own hand and recording voyages made between 1614 and 1619 to Siam and Cochin China, while the library's earliest acquisition of a Japanese printed book was in 1629. It is not known when this shuinjo arrived in the library, nor where it came from, but it was certainly there in 1680 when a list of its manuscripts was compiled. It was evidently not understood and in the seventeenth century it was referred to as both an edict by the king of Japan and 'manuscriptum Chinense'.

MS. Jap. b. 2

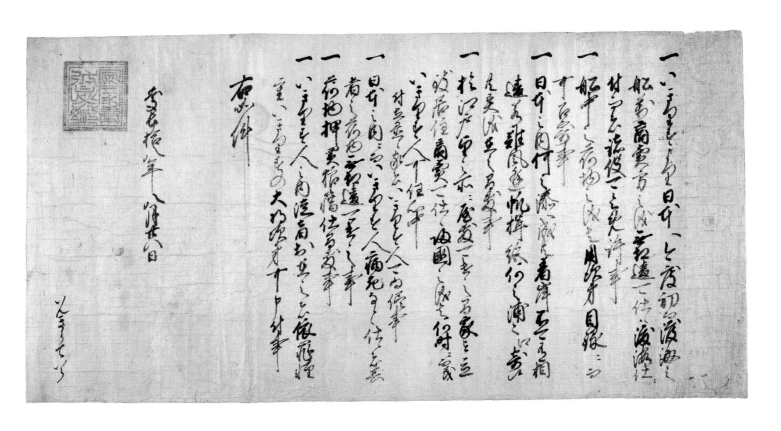

一、□□□□□日中□□夜初□渡海□
　舩□商賣方□□□二船遠□仕、渡海仕
　□□□□送役□□免許事

一、舩中□商物□□□関所手形渡□
　□□□候事

一、日中□自付□□□□□着岸□□□相
　遠□難風逢□帆柱□□□浦□□□
　□□□□□□□事

一、□□□□□□舟□□□家□□□
　□□□□商賣一□□西國□□□□
　□□□□人仕候事

一、□□□□□□□□□□人仕候事

一、日中□商□□□□人□痛□□□
　□□□□□遠一□□□事

一、□地押買狼藉仕□□事

一、□□□□□南□□□□□□□
　□□□□大□□十□□事

　　　　右之件

　　慶長拾年八月廿□日

A dying Mughal courtier

Naturalistic portraiture flourished in India during the Mughal period under the Emperor Jahangir, successor to Akbar (see p. 128), who reigned from 1605 to 1627. Recognizably distinct individuals replaced idealized depictions. This 1618 portrayal of a man at death's door, which came to the Bodleian in 1844, has been called 'one of the most famous of all Mughal portraits'. Restrained in its colours and design, it depicts a former courtier, 'Inayat Khan, wasted by an addiction to opium and to alcohol, on the day before his death. He had asked to visit Jahangir to seek leave to journey to Agra, and the emperor was so astonished at his condition that he ordered this portrait, which has been attributed to Balchand, to be made. A preliminary brush-drawing for this chill picture of ultimate resignation is in the Boston Museum of Fine Arts. The finished version came to Oxford when the Bodleian purchased the collections formed in India and Persia by the diplomat Sir Gore Ouseley and his brother Sir William Ouseley in the nineteenth century.

MS. Ouseley Add. 171, fol. 4v

James I's gifts

In 1620 Oxford University took the decision to embellish
the inner face of the recently completed tower over the
main gateway to its Schools Quadrangle with a statue of
King James I. The king, a scholarly man who had knighted
Sir Thomas Bodley, visited the Bodleian on more than one
occasion. On his first visit in 1605 he is reputed to have
said that 'were it his fate at any time to be a captive, he
would wish to be shut up ... in this place as his prison, to
be bound with its chains, and to consume his days among
its books as his fellows in captivity'. He also apparently
made an offer (never realized) to give Sir Thomas the pick
of any books from the royal libraries.

The statue, made some fifteen years after this visit and seven years after Sir Thomas's death, depicts the king in a less expansive mood. Probably the work of a Yorkshire sculptor, John Clark, and originally coloured, it shows the king presenting copies of his own collected works to, on his left, the university, and, on his right, Fame blowing a trumpet. On the covers of the books are the words 'Haec habeo quae scripsi. Haec habeo quae dedi.' ('These things I have which I have written. These things I have which I have given.')

King James did indeed present the library with two copies of his collected *Works* translated into Latin. The first is a copy of the 1619 issue, bound in olive-green morocco. It is signed by the king and has a flowery inscription by his secretary of state, Sir Robert Naunton.

The second, also signed by the king, is the 1620 issue and it too has a flattering inscription, by Naunton's successor as secretary, Sir George Calvert. This copy is altogether grander, clothed by the royal binder John Bateman in a cover of red velvet, with leather onlays tooled in gilt with the royal arms. It was carried to Oxford by Patrick Young, the librarian at St James's Palace, received at a special convocation in St Mary's church and then carried in a solemn procession led by the vice-chancellor and twenty-four doctors in scarlet gowns to its permanent home in the Bodleian.

James I on the Tower of the Five Orders; Arch. A c.3 (1619), binding; Arch. A b.3 (1620) inscription and binding

A fruit-grower's guidebook

The manuscript from which this illustration comes is undated, but may be assigned to the years between 1620 and 1640. It is not a great work of art nor was it intended to be a showpiece of the skills of a botanical illustrator. Its naïve paintings of various fruits seem to be intended as a guide for gardeners on how to recognize varieties of fruit and to give an idea of their colouring, their size and the date on which they might be expected to ripen. The paintings were bound in their present form by Elias Ashmole (1617–1692) and the volume came to the University of Oxford on his death, along with his great collection of curiosities that formed England's first public museum: the Ashmolean. It moved to the Bodleian Library in 1860 when a rationalization of the collections in the two institutions separated books, manuscripts and papers from museum objects, pictures and coins.

The compiler of the guide is unknown. When first catalogued in 1697 it was simply called 'A Book of Fruit Trees with their Fruits, drawn in Colours, about the year 1640', but when in 1845 the catalogue of Elias Ashmole's library collection was published it was called 'The Tradescant's Orchard', and it has been referred to by that name ever since. Ashmole had acquired the collection of rarities built up at Lambeth by the plantsmen and gardeners John Tradescant the Elder (c.1570–1638) and his son John Tradescant the Younger (1608–1662), but there is no direct evidence to connect them with these paintings save for a note on that of the amber plum 'which J. T as I take it brought out of France and groueth at Hatfield'. The elder Tradescant had overseen the gardeners, and travelled on the continent of Europe collecting plants, for the first earl of Salisbury at Hatfield House from 1610 to 1614.

Many of the paintings are tricked out with birds, insects, caterpillars, spiders, butterflies, squirrels and frogs, as in the case of the queen mother plum shown here. All together the collection depicts an early apple, two varieties of apricot, ten varieties of cherry, a gooseberry, six pears, twelve peaches, five nectarines, four grapevines, two quinces, a strawberry, four pears and twenty-three plums (including two damsons and a bullace). The whole group constitutes a charming link to practical gardeners in the first half of the seventeenth century.

MS. Ashmole 1461, fol. 47

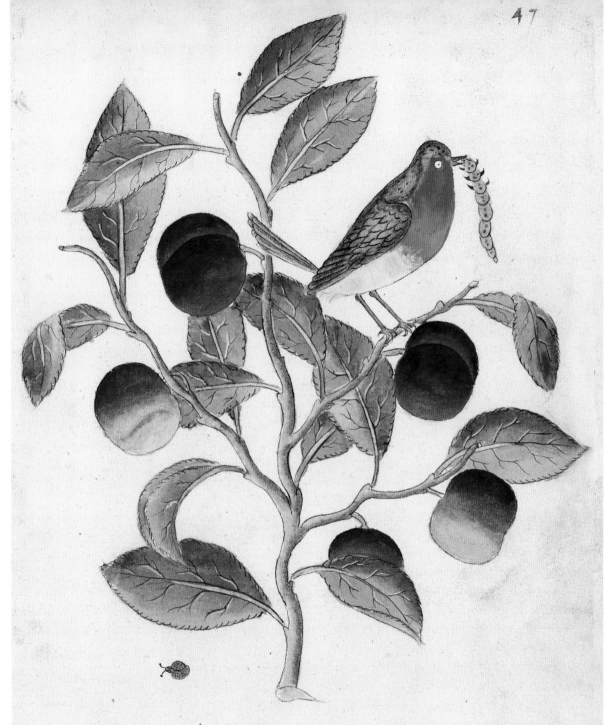

The guene mother plum
August 14
or muskedin or cherry

Regulating the University, 1636

The archives of the University of Oxford, which had been independently overseen by their own keeper since 1634, were brought within the administration of the Bodleian Library in 2010. Among them one of the most impressive documents, and certainly the heaviest, is the *codex authenticus* of the Laudian Code of Statutes of 1636. These statutes, under which the university was governed for over two hundred years, emerged from the seven-year-long deliberation of a delegacy appointed in 1629 on the initiative of Charles I's close adviser William Laud, president of St John's College from 1611 to 1621, who regarded the university as 'extremely sunk from all discipline, and fallen into licentiousness'. Laud's election as chancellor of the university in 1630 and appointment as archbishop of Canterbury in 1632 put him in a position from which he could closely monitor and supervise the reform of the university's statutes, and the *codex authenticus* demonstrates both how close this control was and how magisterial the outcome was intended to be.

The codex is contained in a large and weighty leather-bound volume with the royal arms on the top and bottom boards. It measures some 47 x 32cm and is about 10cm thick. It is closed with blue silk ties and all its edges are gilt. The statutes themselves are beautifully penned on two hundred leaves of heavy vellum, the scribe, William Ball, having been paid over £33 for his work. The title page is signed by Laud, the table of contents is signed by Laud, within the statutes each title is signed by Laud, and prefacing them are three folios containing four columns listing 138 places where the scribe had had to make a correction: each of these columns is also signed by Laud.

The statutes regulate all aspects of university life from the structure of government, teaching and residence to, for instance, the dress and hairstyles of its members. Title XIV, section I, illustrated here, forbids ringlets (*cincinnos*) and excessively flowing locks (*comam nimis promissam*).

Bound in with the statutes are three further documents: a deed of confirmation and ratification, dated 2 June 1636, signed by Laud, suspended from which, in silver skippets, are his seals as archbishop and chancellor of the university; letters patent of King Charles I confirming the statues, dated 3 June, signed Carolus R, with a fine portrait in the initial letter C (illustrated on p. 155), and sealed with the Great Seal in a hinged silver skippet; and a further document of confirmation, dated 22 June, signed by the dean and four canons of Christ Church and twenty-six heads of colleges and halls. Eight further leaves record additions to the statutes from 1640 to 1758.

OU Archives WPγ/25c/1 fol. 92

TIT. XIV.   *DE VESTITU ET HABITU SCHOLASTICO.*

§. 1. De Vestitu Præfectorum, Sociorum & Scholarium Collegiorum; Et de modo in Vestibus seruando a cæteris.

STATVTVM est, quod omnes Præfecti, Collegiorum Socij et Scholares, necnon omnes Sacris Ordinibus initiati, prout Clericos licet, vestiantur; et ea observent, quæ Canonicis sanctionibus præcipiuntur. [1] B. III. b.

Quodque alij omnes (exceptis solis Baronum in Superiore Parliamenti Domo suffragij ius habentium) vestibus coloris nigri aut subfusci se assuefaciant; nec, quæ fastum aut luxum præ se ferunt, imitentur; sed ab ijs procul absint. [2] KK. 4. b.

Insuper ab absurdo illo et fastuoso, publice in sericis ambulandi more, abstinere compellantur. [3] N. 146 b.

Etiam in capillitio modus esto; nec cincinnos, aut comam nimis promissam alant. Si quis vero in præmissis deliquerit, si Graduatus fuerit, pænâ 6 et 8. plectatur, toties quoties. Si non Graduatus (si per ætatem conveniat) pænâ corporali; sin minus arbitrio Vicecancellarij vel Procuratorum (ita vt summam præfatam non excedant) coerceatur. Quas mulctas, partim ad Vniversitatis, partim ad proprios vsus exigendi Procuratores potestatem habeant.

§. 2. De reprimendis et puniendis novos et insolitos Habitus invehentibus.

STATVTVM est, quod, si contingat, aliquos, in vestitu novos et insolitos Habitus introducere, Vicecancellarius, et Præfecti Collegiorum et Aularum, habita inter se deliberatione, de eodem sententias suas in medium proferant.

Deinde Vicecancellarius Sartoribus siue Sartoribus vestiariis, huiusmodi vestes conficiendi potestate interdicat; et Præfecti suis singuli Scholaribus huiusmodi vestimentorum vsu interdicant.

Si maius remedio vitium invaluerit, nec pænis, quamvis seueris (quas secundum qualitatem delicti pro arbitrio infliget Vicecancellarius) morbi pertinacia expugnari possit, post tres monitiones, vel pænas ordinarias ter inflictas ad Bannitionem procedere licebit.

§. 3. Habitus Academici, singulis Gradibus et Facultatibus competentes.

STATVTVM est, quod non graduati, quotquot alicuius Collegij Socij, Probationarij, Scholares, Capellani, Clerici, Choristæ, denique quotquot de Fundatione Collegij cuiusvis fuerint, Studentes insuper Ædis Christi, quoties in publicum in Vniversitate prodeunt, Togis laxe manicatis, et Pileis quadratis induti incedant. [1] B. 119. N. 120.

Quotquot

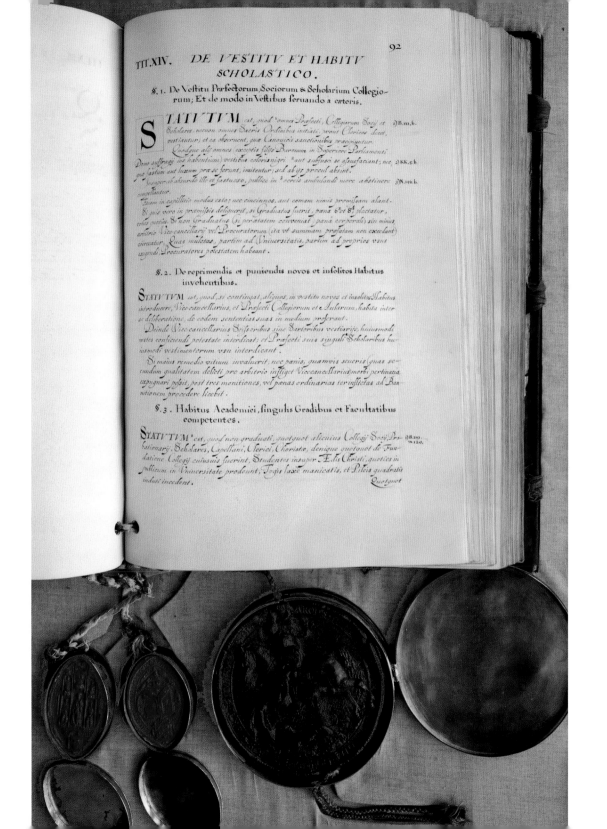

Bronzes by Hubert Le Sueur

Two of the Bodleian Library's greatest benefactors in the first forty years of its existence were successively chancellor of the University of Oxford: William Herbert, third earl of Pembroke, and Archbishop William Laud. Their gifts of Greek manuscripts in particular (including in Pembroke's case 244 such volumes in the Barocci collection) established the library's pre-eminence in Great Britain in that field. Laud's gifts in the 1630s included some ninety-four such manuscripts and reinforced the earl's view, expressed when he prevented the break-up of the Barocci collection, which had been put together in Venice, 'that they would be of more use to the Church in being kept united in some publick Librarye then scattered in particular hands'.

Laud also purchased and presented to the library in 1636 a bronze bust by Hubert Le Sueur of King Charles I, Laud's master, who had attracted the sculptor to England in 1625. Laud requested that the bust be placed with the manuscripts which he himself had given and which had arrived the year before, so that its presence would deter anyone intending to harm them. In 1641 it was placed in a niche on the north side of the entrance to Duke Humfrey's Library, directly across the aisle from the bust of Sir Thomas Bodley, where it still remains (see p. 11).

At much the same time Le Sueur was at work on a posthumous, larger-than-life, full-length statue of the earl of Pembroke (pictured), who had died in 1630. Probably commissioned by Pembroke's brother, the statue stood at the earl's family home at Wilton in Wiltshire until 1723, when it was presented to the University of Oxford by his descendant and great-nephew the seventh earl. It was placed in the Picture Gallery, now the library's Upper Reading Room, where it stood until moved in 1951 to its present position in the Old Schools Quadrangle in front of the main entrance to the Old Library.

The library's second Benefactors' Register records the gift of the statue under the date 1724, in which year also gifts of books were recorded from the poet Alexander Pope and the chancellor of the Exchequer Robert Walpole. It also notes the gift of an intricately carved ostrich egg (*Ovum Struthocameli*).

Statue of Earl of Pembroke

Charles I's request refused

The year after the bust of King Charles I was placed in Duke Humfrey's Library (see p.11), civil war broke out in England and for the next four years, from 1642 to 1646, Oxford became the royalist headquarters. The king moved into Christ Church, where he occupied the Deanery – displacing the dean, Dr Samuel Fell.

On 30 December 1645, with his fortunes at a low ebb, King Charles found time for reading and had this note sent to Fell, who was then the university's vice-chancellor, in which he ordered that a book from the Bodleian be brought to him. The note was then passed on by the vice-chancellor to Bodley's Librarian, John Rous, with Fell's added note: 'His Majestyes use is in commaund to us'.

The book in question was the *Histoire Universelle du Sieur D'Aubigné*, a work in three folio volumes by Theodore-Agrippa d'Aubigné (1552–1630), the Huguenot soldier, poet and historian. The volumes were published at the Château de Maillé in 1616, 1618 and 1620 and cover the French religious wars in the period 1553–1602. The book was indeed in the Bodleian (three volumes bound as two) but the request confronted Bodley's Librarian with a problem. He had sworn to enforce the library's statutes, under which no book might be lent. He therefore went to see the king, taking the statutes with him. According to Rous's successor, Thomas Barlow, the king – having read the statutes – appreciated Rous's point of view and 'would not have the booke, nor permit it to be taken out of the library, saying it was fit that the will and statutes of the pious founder should be religiously observed'.

A 3.8-9 Jur; MS. Clarendon 91, fol. 18r; OU Archives WP γ/25c/1, fol.205r

Carolus R.

CAROLUS
dei gratia Anglie Scotie ffrancie et Hibernie Rex fidei defensor; Vniuis ad quos presentes litere peruenerint, Salutem; Cum ob multiplicem in celeberrima vniuersitate Oxon Statutor varietatem atqs incertam que per antecessa betnsta exerevit congeriem tam obseruationis cor quam interpretationis difficultates non exigue nec infrequentes dudum exceterunt negs fuerint ipsa recentiori euo batus accommoda omnia aut consentanea. Cui malo ut tempestiua Reformationis medela adhibeetur atqs ut noua eiatu, vbi reg epigtegt, que regnimi ditte Vuiuersitatis momms vtilisa souent constituerentur Nos vst smmio quo dictam Vniuersitatem

---

B. 2061   December 30. 1645.   18

Deliver unto the bearer hereof, for the
present use of his Maiesty, a Booke
Intituled Histoire Vniuerselle du Sieur
D'Aubigné: and this shall be your

warrant.

His maiesties vt: & jn Commaund vm
Edw: Nicolas.

II***

The Bay Psalm Book and
The Massachusetts Bible

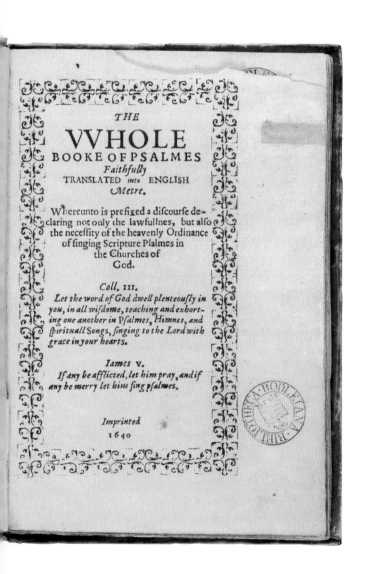

In 1638 Stephen Day, a locksmith from Cambridge, England, was financed by an Anglican minister from Surrey, Joseph Glover, to travel with him to Cambridge, Massachusetts. Glover took with him the equipment and paper necessary to set up a printing press there. He, however, died aboard ship. Day completed the voyage with Glover's widow and his own family, and on arrival assumed the management of the press, starting to print in 1639. The first complete book printed by him, and therefore the first book printed in British colonial America, was *The Whole Booke of Psalmes Faithfully Translated into English Metre* published in 1640 and known today as the Bay Psalm Book. Originally published in 1,700 copies, only 11 are known to survive, and the copy in the Bodleian Library is the only one outside North America. It came in 1736 with the collection of some 467 manuscripts and over 900 printed books amassed by the antiquary Thomas Tanner, bishop of St Asaph.

The psalms were rendered into metrical verse by a group of divines in New England that included John Eliot – a Cambridge puritan known as the Apostle to the Indians. By 1661 Eliot had translated the New Testament into the language of the Massachusetts Native Americans and in 1663 the Old Testament joined it to make the first Bible printed in North America and the first printed in a language spoken by natives of that

continent. By that date a new press had been sent over from England and, as the title page shows, typesetting and spelling had progressed beyond their amateurish beginnings.

The Bodleian copy of this rare work was presented in 1667 by the overseers of Harvard College to Ralph Freke of Hannington, Wiltshire, a retired lawyer and country squire, who was, in the words of an inscription in the book 'A nobl Benefactor to the abovesayd colledg.' A year later, perhaps baffled by the strange language, he presented it to the Bodleian Library in his old university.

Arch. G e.31 and 4° E 2 Th., title pages

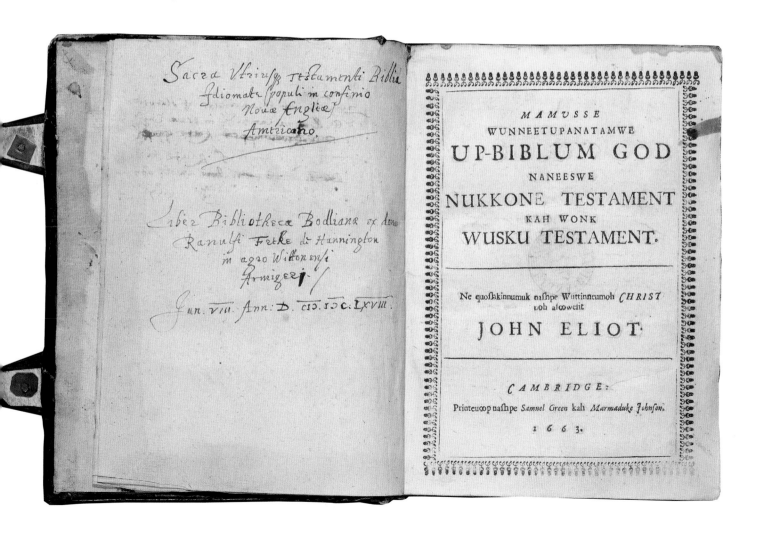

Seventeenth-century rebels

These two sheets of paper from the seventeenth century spotlight critical moments in the lives of two very different personalities in English society in times of rebellion.

The first survives in the papers of Sir John Bankes, who was Charles I's attorney-general during the years from 1634 to 1640. The papers were discovered in the estate office of the Bledisloe family at Lydney Park in Gloucestershire in 1949 and were bought by the library in 1959. This single sheet – one among thousands – records the examination on 17 May 1638, before Bankes and the solicitor-general Sir Edward Littleton, of the notorious agitator, pamphleteer and Leveller John Lilburne (1615?–1657). Lilburne had been convicted of distributing seditious pamphlets and, having refused to take an oath in court, he was whipped through the streets of London and pilloried but, as this examination shows, remained incorrigible, continuing to distribute from the pillory the banned works of John Bastwicke and refusing to disclose the source of them. Moreover, he refused to acknowledge the authority of bishops, declaring that 'theyr calling was soe farre from being from God that he would maintaine that theyr calling, power and authoritie was from the devill'. The examination ends, in Lilburne's own hand, with the words '& this I will sealle with my dearest blood. P[er] me John: Lilburne'.

Lilburne spent the rest of his life stubbornly at odds with authority, and died a pauper and virtually friendless.

The second was written almost half a century later and came to the Bodleian Library in 1755 in the vast collection left to it by Richard Rawlinson. It bears the signature of James Scott, duke of Monmouth and of Buccleugh, the illegitimate son of the future King Charles II of England and Lucy Walter. On the accession of the Roman Catholic James II following Charles II's death in 1685, Monmouth raised a rebellion against him. He was defeated at Sedgemoor and, on 15 July before being executed, he signed this letter acknowledging his illegitimacy and begging that 'the King who is now will not let my Children suffer on this Account'.

MS. Bankes 18/3; MS. Rawl. A. 139b, fol. 8r

The examination of John Lilburne taken the
17th day of may 14 Caroli R. before his
maiesties Attorney and Soliciter generall.

He saith that being upon the pillorie he
affirmed concerning the Bishops and theire
calling that they yet in the tyme of King
Elizabeth and King James to challenge theire
calling from the King, but in the reigne
of that noble doctor Dr Bastwick they
renounced the kings authoritie, and said
theire calling was not from the King, but
from God, and he further said that theire
calling was soe farre from being from God
that he would maintaine that theire calling
power and authoritie was from the divill, and
he confesseth that while he stood upon the
pillorie he scattered three bookes of Doctor
Bastwickes amongst the people namely his
Letanie, his answeare to mr Attorney his
information, and a third booke in which
certaine particulars to some objections made
against his Letanie, and being demaunded where
he had those bookes and of whom he would
give noe other informacion but that he
was unwilling to tell it. Who will seale
with my dearest blood of me Jhn: Lilbourne

Jo: Bankes
Edward Littleton.

I declare yt ye Title of King was forct upon
mee & yt it was very much contrary to my opinion
when I was proclaimd. For ye Satisfaction of
the world I doe declare that ye late King told me that
Hee was never married to my Mother.

Haveing declard this I hope yt the King who is now
will not let my Children suffer on this Account. And to
this I put my hand this fifteenth day of July
1685.   MONMOUTH

I declard by himselfe & signd in the presence of us.

Fran: Elis.
Tho: BatheWells
Tho: Tenison
Geo Hooper

The Drake Chair

The Bodleian, prior to the foundation of the Ashmolean Museum in 1683, was Oxford University's 'Cabinet of Curiosities' as well as its central library. As such it became the repository for artefacts of all sorts, ranging from Guy Fawkes's lantern to mummified bodies, architectural models, pictures and coins. Almost all, save for a number of portraits, have now been dispersed to other university institutions, but one principal one remains in the library on public display: the Drake Chair.

Sir Francis Drake, like Sir Thomas Bodley, was a Devonian. The two men were contemporaries and must at least have known each other as fellow members of parliament in the 1580s, following Drake's return from his circumnavigation of the world in 1581. Queen Elizabeth had knighted Drake at Deptford on board the *Golden Hind*, for which a special dry dock was constructed. Over the years, however, the ship decayed and John Davies, storekeeper at Deptford Dockyard, arranged for her final breaking-up. From the timbers he had an armchair made which in 1662 he presented to the Bodleian. At least three other similar, though cruder, chairs are recorded, but for this one the poet Abraham Cowley – whose brother worked with Davies at the dockyard – agreed to provide commemorative verses in both Latin and English. These are engraved on metal plates and attached to the chair. The English verse reads:

To this great Ship which round the Globe has run,
And matcht in Race the Chariot of the Sun,
This Pythagorean Ship (for it may claime
Without Presumption so deserv'd a Name,
By knowledge once, and transformation now)
In her new shape, this sacred Port allow.
Drake & his Ship, could not have wisht from Fate
A more blest Station, or more blest Estate.
For Lo! a Seate of endles Rest is giv'n
To her in Oxford, and to him in Heav'n.

A royal conversation

Edward Hyde, first earl of Clarendon (1609–1674) was, until his downfall in 1667, a trusted adviser and confidant of King Charles II, whose restoration to the throne of England in 1660 he had successfully negotiated. During the years from the Restoration to 1667 he was also chancellor of the University of Oxford and is known to have visited the Bodleian Library then. His name lives on in perpetuity in the Clarendon Building (p. 22) facing Broad Street. Nicholas Hawksmoor's first completed Oxford building was erected in 1712–13 to house the university's printing house and was funded almost entirely from the profits of Clarendon's *History of the Great Rebellion*, which the university first published in 1702–03. The building now houses the administrative headquarters of the Bodleian Library and the other university libraries associated with it in the Bodleian Libraries system.

When the large archive of Lord Clarendon's papers was given to Oxford University by his descendants in 1759, almost a century after his death, the gift catapulted the Bodleian into the forefront of centres for the study of seventeenth-century British history. From this archive one small fragment is shown as illustrating the closeness of king and chancellor, who could exchange information and humour even during a Privy Council meeting when private conversations were forbidden. It is a note, one of some ninety such scraps to have survived in the archive, that passed between the two men during such a meeting. The king begins it by asking Clarendon when he can escape from matters of state to go to Tunbridge for a night or two, to which Clarendon replies that two nights during the following week are a possibility and advises him to go 'with a light Trayne'. Charles then writes that he will take 'nothing but my night bag', but when Clarendon insists that he must not go 'without 40 or 50 horse' the king replies 'I counte that parte of my night bag'.

MS. Clarendon 100, fol. 54r

I would willingly make a visite to my sister at
tunbridge for a night, or two at farthest, when do
you thinke I can ~~~~ best spare that time?

I know no reason why you may not for such
a tyme, (2. nights) $\overline{w}$ the next weeke,
about Wensday, or Thursday, and whave tyme
enough for the adiournment: which you ought
to be the weeke following.

I suppose you will goe with a light
Traine.

I intend to take nothing but my night bag.

yos, you will not goe without 40. or 50.
horse.

I counte that parte of my night bag.

The first opera in English

This unassuming manuscript book written in about 1670, lacking a title page, bound in goatskin and with a spine-label stating simply 'An Opera in English', is of very great importance in the history of musical performance in the British Isles. It contains the full score of the opera *Erismena* by Piero Francesco Cavalli (1602–1676) – a work first performed in Venice in 1655. It is unique in that it is not only the earliest surviving score of an opera in English but also the earliest known translation of an Italian libretto into English. No evidence exists to show when, or indeed if, it was performed in England in the 1670s. Italian opera did not become popular in England until some thirty years later, though this score was clearly prepared with performance in mind. The original Italian score, which survives in Venice, has no prologue. Prologues were often written and composed for particular occasions and that which exists in this manuscript features a different cast of characters from those in the Italian printed libretti. It was almost certainly written by Englishmen for an English production. John Evelyn notes in his diary in January 1674 that he 'saw an Italian Opera in musique, the first that had been in England of this kind'. Cavalli was the leading Italian opera composer of the time and Evelyn may very well have seen *Erismena*.

The manuscript came up for sale in London in 2009 and the Bodleian Library, aided by grants from many charitable sources, was able to prevent its export and acquire it for £85,000. It is no stranger to the University of Oxford. In the eighteenth century it belonged to William and Philip Hayes, successive professors of music from 1741 to 1797, whose library was sold in the latter year.

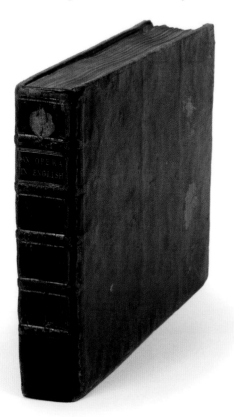

MS. Mus. d. 282, binding and fols. 3v–4r

John Locke, philosopher and civil servant

This portrait of John Locke (1632–1704), given to the University of Oxford by the painter Thomas Gibson in 1733, hangs in the Bodleian Library. It shows him with his right hand resting on a copy of his most famous philosophical work, *An Essay concerning Human Understanding*, published in 1690. The library also owns an extensive collection of Locke's manuscripts and letters bought from the earl of Lovelace in 1947 and also that part of Locke's personal library known as the King Moiety, which was acquired by the American collector Paul Mellon and given by him to the Bodleian along with further manuscripts in 1978.

John Locke's enduring fame is as a philosopher whose views on the basis of power and government shaped subsequent interpretations of liberal democracy in both Europe and America. His formal education at Oxford, however, was more concerned with experimental science and medicine, and with his qualifications in these in 1667 he entered the service of Anthony Ashley Cooper, later first earl of Shaftesbury, for whom he acted as resident physician and secretary. As chancellor of the exchequer (and later lord chancellor), Shaftesbury persuaded King Charles II to create the Board of Trade and Plantations, of which Locke became secretary, serving in the same capacity for the lords proprietors of the Carolinas. He was assiduous in these offices and

surviving in the papers in the Bodleian are notes taken at their meetings which show him gathering and collating information for the government on the colonists and on trade. The notes reproduced here, made at a meeting of the lords proprietors on 26 December 1674, illustrate the plight and the needs of a small group, principally male, attempting to gain a foothold and to breed in the new American territories. Along with nails, stockings, and shoes, they 'desire women'.

LP 186, MS. Locke c. 30, fols 6v – 7r

12

A Tempest in the begining of
August destroyd a great pt of their
Corne & Tobaco 1
An well stored with corne. 2
Can scarce afford their tobaco for 6d pr tt
Desire small nailes. 2
Designe Tobaco & pipe staves 2.
~~Desire whole boat load~~
Desire interest may be remitted 3.
Cannot settle in townes within 60 miles
of the sea 4.
Wold pay in pipe staves 5
Desire a supply of Cattle clothes & tooles 6.
particularly better stockings & shoes, white
linin, better clothes for mosters of familys
blanketts & rugs 7.
2. Whether the publique seale may be
applied to certificats els they desire another 8
Desire a minister & Surgeon 9.
Since may 23 but one small family & 2
single men have arived there Except mr

---

percival they are but 170 men, &
the single men ready to be gon or fast as
they can 9
Desire women 10

Extract   The peoples address to
the Governor & Grand Council
22 Dec 74

Desire remission of Interest, forbearance
of debts & to pay in pipe staves 3
Desire Clothes tooles nailes & cattle 4
will goe upon any commodity y LP py
shall direct.

Extract   Joseph Wel to ye Ls
py
22 Sept 74

Thanks for his patents 1
way chosen governor by yr people upon the
death of Sr Jo: Yeamans 2
Servants when out of their time & debtors when
clear are ready to be gon because of yr want of
supplys 2
Desire & ship ith people espetially rich men

Samuel Pepys

Samuel Pepys (1633–1703) is generally best known as a great English diarist. Yet his diary, originally meant for his eyes only, covers a mere nine years (1660–69) in the life of a busy young man who was to live beyond his seventieth birthday. During this long life he was known as a very learned man, an early fellow of the Royal Society, the collector of a large library, and principally as a skilled naval administrator under the Stuart kings Charles II and James II. In his will he left his library and archive to a nephew with instructions that upon the nephew's death it should go to Magdalene College, Cambridge, where he had been an undergraduate. However, a mass of papers – including many concerned with his work as an administrator – became separated and were acquired by Pepys's near-contemporary Richard Rawlinson whose collections came to the Bodleian Library following his death in 1755.

These papers, gathered up into over a hundred bound volumes, are important, supplementing those at Magdalene College, Cambridge, in throwing light on the administration of the navy and other matters in the second half of the seventeenth century. The one illustrated here, however, also shows how sometimes not only a document's content but also its very shape can add a historical dimension by illuminating the motivation and method of the person who wrote it.

In April 1688 Pepys, as secretary for naval affairs, had a meeting with King James II to discuss maritime matters. Ahead of the meeting he made lists of points for discussion on two sheets of paper to use discreetly as an aide-memoire. These two sheets were folded, concertina fashion, into eight pages making an oblong pad which could be easily slipped in and out of a pocket or a sleeve cuff and consulted unobtrusively during the meeting.

In less than a year, with the arrival of King William III, this highly competent civil servant and meticulous preparer of meetings had lost his job, but he took care that documents such as this one went with him into his own library.

MS. Rawl. A. 170, fol. 217r

Left panel

See that his Ma.ⁱᵉˢ present
proposicōn to mee, of haveing
his Navy (since thus, as he is
pleasd to esteeme it, recover'd)
restored to its old Constitucōn,
& his old Officers taken back
againe thereinto, viz. Controll.
Survey. & ye 2 Acts; with the
addicōn. Provision (borrow'd
as his Ma.ⁱʸ is pleasd to tell mee, from
ye present practice of France)
of ye effectuall execucōn of theyr
Offices for ye time to come, viz.
of Inspectōn.— Persons fitly
qualify'd by theyr universall
& approved knowledge, & ——
empower'd by Authō-
rity from ye King, to inspect
& controll ye Performances of
all Offices great & small, & ——
-tify or report to his Ma.ⁱʸ what-
-ever hee shall finde amisse,
or judge improveable therein.
Giving this his Ma.ⁱˢ Proposicōn
w.ᵗʰ this his addicōn. Cau——
-tion

Middle panel

-tion may (uppon my full weigh-
-ing ye whole) not only safely
& without any excepcōn of Change
but with advantage, bee putt
in execution; & that ye person
proposed by ye King, viz. S.ʳ A.
Deane, is ye only Man I know
at this time qualify'd for that
part of this Inspectorshᵖ. w.ᶜʰ
relates to ye Workes & Stores,
& Mr. Hewer to ye Accounts.

   Butt submitt to his Ma.ⁱʸ
ye consideracōns of ye expedi-
-ency of haveing ye following
workes first dispatched. viz.

1 --- The making up all the
   old Accounts.

2 --- The finishing ye Workes
   & accounts thereof now be-
   -fore us upon ye Proporcōn.

3 --- The review, perfecting,
   & establishing a Body of In-
   -struccōns upon ye old Foot
   of ye Navy, for ye Guidance
   of all its Officers.

All attaineable w.ᵗʰ ye ——
this
in ye Present Yeare.

Right panel

Navy. cont
Generall Consider.

Its Science ye most extensive
of any. viz. Comoditys
                    Trades.
                    Provisions.
Climates.   Ship-building.
Accounts.   Discipline.
Thrift.   Ship Wind.
Seamanꝭp.   Tides.
Navigacōn.   Seas.
Sea-Laws.   &c.

Noe one Man qualify'd for
all.
Nor fitt to bee trusted
alone.
Therefore ye old Constitucōn
provided for all, & by
a Plurality properly
qualify'd.
With Instructions sui——
-table

Ethiopian miniatures

The two manuscripts which carry these striking naïve illustrations are from Ethiopia and form part of a collection of over fifty Ethiopic items bequeathed to the Bodleian Library by a great twentieth-century bibliophile Dr Bent Juel-Jensen (1922–2006), Oxford University Medical Officer and collector in many fields including, besides Ethiopic manuscripts and crucifixes, coins, early and rare books from Denmark (his native country), and English literature of the sixteenth and seventeenth centuries, in all of which fields he greatly enriched the collections of the university by gift and bequest.

The charming and accomplished painting shown opposite is one of 33 large miniatures (and the only one filling an entire page) which illustrate a seventeenth-century manuscript, in its original binding, of the second (winter) part of the Ethiopic Golden Legend or Synkessar. It depicts the Nativity of Jesus Christ. Mary and Joseph are shown displaying the baby to the Magi who kneel and present gifts in the company of two oxen, an ass, a pig and two sheep. Above them an upper row of angels play musical instruments and a lower row blow trumpets through a bank of fluffy clouds. When this manuscript was sold at Sotheby's on 1 December 1987 the illustrations were thought to be contemporary with the seventeenth-century text which they enliven. Dr Juel-Jensen, however, subsequently proved that they are twentieth-century forgeries (though no less accomplished for that) sometimes added over the original script, and the book was recalled. The forger has not been identified. Dr Juel-Jensen acquired the manuscript in 1993.

Dating from the second quarter of the eighteenth century and originating at Gondar, the manuscript shown overleaf, in its original binding of blind-stamped goatskin over wooden boards, tells the story of the supposed life, miracles, and martyrdom of St George. Its 38 miniatures (29 of which occupy a full page) illustrate how St George became a Christian, gave away his possessions, and freed his slaves. Seeking from the king, Dudeyanos, the right to succeed his father as governor of a province, he refused the king's order to worship idols and was as a consequence tortured and martyred. Most of the pictures depict the gruesome tortures to which George was subjected but this one portrays the saint on a richly caparisoned white horse in the act for which he is most widely celebrated in the west – slaying a dragon – in front of a church and other Gondarene buildings.

MS. Aeth.b.6 (Arch O.b.23), fol. 105v; MS. Aeth.b.4 (Arch.O.b.22) fols. 13v – 14r

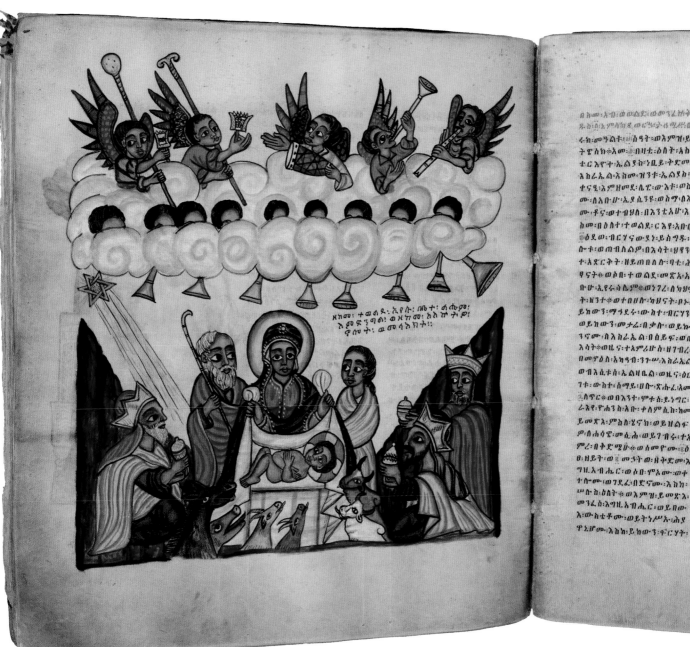

ዘከመ፡ ተወልደ፡ ኢየሱ፡ ዜተ፡ ሐሐያዋ፡
ዘ፡ ምድ፡ ንግዳ፡ ወ፡ ዘ፡ ከመ፡ እ፡ ስ፡ ኮ፡ ት፡ ሆ፡
እ፡ ሱ፡ ኮ፡ ት፡ ወ፡ መ፡ ሳ፡ እ፡ ክ፡ ት፡፡

በ፡ እከ፡ መ፡ አ፡ ብ፡ ወ፡ ወ፡ ልድ፡ ወ፡ መ፡ ንፈ፡ ቅዱ፡
ዱ፡ እ፡ ስ፡ ብ፡ ሐ፡ ት፡ ምስጋ፡ ል፡ ወ፡ መ፡ ና፡ ሁ፡ ላ፡ ዊ፡
ፈ፡ መ፡ ዓ፡ ል፡ ት፡፡ ሀ፡ ስ፡ ጋ፡ ት፡ ወ፡ ለ፡ ም፡ ህ፡ ይ፡
ት፡ እ፡ ስ፡ ክ፡ እ፡ ተ፡ ዘ፡ በ፡ ዛ፡ ቲ፡ ዕ፡ ል፡ ት፡
ተ፡ እ፡ ር፡ ክ፡ ት፡ ዘ፡ ሐ፡ መ፡ በ፡ ለ፡ ሱ፡ ባ፡ ሕ
ዓ፡ ና፡ ት፡ ወ፡ ስ፡ በ፡ ተ፡ ወ፡ ል፡ ደ፡ መ፡ ድ፡ እ
ቡ፡ እ፡ ኢ፡ የ፡ ሱ፡ ል፡ ም፡ ወ፡ ነ፡ ገ፡ ረ፡ ለ፡ ክ፡ ህ፡
ት፡ ዘ፡ ክ፡ ን፡ ት፡ ወ፡ ተ፡ ብ፡ በ፡ በ፡ ከ፡ ና፡ ት፡ ቡ፡
ይ፡ ክ፡ ው፡ ን፡ ማ፡ ዲ፡ ነ፡ ው፡ ክ፡ ት፡ በ፡ ር፡ ሃ፡ ን፡
ወ፡ ይ፡ ክ፡ ው፡ ን፡ መ፡ ታ፡ ደ፡ በ፡ ካ፡ ሪ፡ ወ፡ ይ፡ ደ፡
ን፡ ጋ፡ ም፡ ስ፡ ከ፡ ራ፡ ል፡ ል፡ በ፡ ሰ፡ ዕ፡ ደ፡ ት፡ ወ፡ ደ
እ፡ ስ፡ ተ፡ ወ፡ ፍ፡ ር፡ ተ፡ እ፡ ም፡ ዝ፡ ሁ፡ ብ፡ ዝ፡
በ፡ መ፡ ዋ፡ ዕ፡ ል፡ አ፡ ከ፡ ና፡ ብ፡ ት፡ ም፡ እ፡ ስ፡ ራ፡ ኤ፡ ል፡
ወ፡ በ፡ ል፡ ቱ፡ ስ፡ ኤ፡ ል፡ ዳ፡ ሌ፡ ወ፡ ል፡ ና፡ ዶ፡
ገ፡ ተ፡ ወ፡ ስ፡ ተ፡ ስ፡ ማ፡ ይ፡ ሆ፡ ወ፡ ድ፡ ስ፡ ረ፡ እ፡ ም፡
እ፡ ጓ፡ ሮ፡ ወ፡ እ፡ ን፡ ዝ፡ ት፡ ም፡ ተ፡ ደ፡ ይ፡ ን፡ ገ፡
ራ፡ እ፡ የ፡ ሃ፡ ን፡ ል፡ አ፡ ብ፡ ወ፡ ቀ፡ ለ፡ ም፡ ሲ፡ ክ፡ ሆ፡ ም፡
ይ፡ መ፡ እ፡ ም፡ ስ፡ ክ፡ ር፡ ኪ፡ ወ፡ ይ፡ ዘ፡ ም፡ ር፡
ም፡ በ፡ ሐ፡ ሳ፡ ዌ፡ መ፡ ሪ፡ ሐ፡ ወ፡ ደ፡ ን፡ ብ፡ ሩ፡ ተ፡ እ
ም፡ በ፡ ተ፡ ዶ፡ ም፡ ዌ፡ እ፡ ን፡ ት፡ ሰ፡ ም፡ ሉ፡ ም፡ ቁ
ዕ፡ ዘ፡ ይ፡ ት፡ ወ፡ መ፡ ታ፡ ት፡ ወ፡ ዘ፡ ፍ፡ ዕ፡ ም፡
ግ፡ ዚ፡ አ፡ ብ፡ ሔ፡ ር፡ ወ፡ ስ፡ ቦ፡ ም፡ ሳ፡ ም፡ ወ፡
ተ፡ ሁ፡ ም፡ ወ፡ ገ፡ ዶ፡ በ፡ ይ፡ ና፡ ው፡ እ፡ ክ
ሱ፡ ል፡ ክ፡ ስ፡ ተ፡ ወ፡ እ፡ ን፡ ም፡ ዝ፡ መ፡ ዶ፡ ል
መ፡ ን፡ ፈ፡ ስ፡ ግ፡ ዚ፡ አ፡ ሔ፡ ር፡ ወ፡ ደ፡ በ
እ፡ ው፡ ክ፡ ቶ፡ ም፡ ወ፡ ደ፡ ት፡ ና፡ ሐ፡ ኡ፡ ሐ፡ ል
ዋ፡ እ፡ ሁ፡ ም፡ እ፡ ን፡ ደ፡ ይ፡ ክ፡ ው፡ ን፡ ፍ፡ ቁ፡ ርት፡

በ፡ ስ፡ ም፡ አ፡ ብ፡ ወ፡ ወ፡ ል፡ ደ፡ ወ፡ መ፡ ንፈ፡ ቅዱ
ዱ፡ እ፡ ስ፡ ብ፡ ሐ፡ ት፡ ም፡ ስ፡ ጋ፡ ል፡ ወ፡ ና፡ ሁ፡ ላ፡ ዊ

ስ፡ ክ፡ ሳ፡ ዘ፡ ም
ወ፡ ደ፡ ም፡ እ፡ መ
ዘ፡ ደ፡ መ፡ ና
ደ፡ ል፡ ጎ፡ ል፡ ት
ኮ፡ ን፡ ጲ፡ ጽ
አ፡ ጉ፡ ዴ፡ ዝ
ር፡ ብ፡ ን፡ ስ፡ ት
ክ፡ ዳ፡ ብ፡ ሕ
ሠ፡ ት፡ ክ፡ ሎ
ግ፡ ለ፡ ዶ፡ ም
ስ፡ ዮ፡ ሐ፡ ለ
ወ፡ ዘ፡ በ፡ ዚ
ት፡ ኢ፡ የ፡ ደ
ለ፡ ና፡ ቀ፡ ዱ
ል፡ ሠ፡ ለ፡ ዝ
ይ፡ በ፡ ሱ፡ ል
ን፡ ተ፡ ዓ፡ ብ
ዓ፡ ል፡ ዚ፡ ው
ት፡ ዶ፡ ው፡ ሐ
ይ፡ ክ፡ ው፡ ን
ጎ፡ ን፡ ክ፡ መ
ሐ፡ ስ፡ ስ፡ ክ
ክ፡ ር፡ ክ፡ ስ፡ ት
ከ፡ ዳ፡ ብ፡ ሐ
እ፡ ክ፡ ቢ፡ ሁ
ጓ፡ እ፡ ክ፡ ለ
ሲ፡ ት፡ ክ፡ ሲ፡ ቢ
ኪ፡ ከ፡ ዘ፡ ለ
ባ፡ እ፡ ስ፡ ሙ፡ መ
ወ፡ ስ፡ ብ፡ ሁ
ዊ፡ ጎ፡ ወ፡ ደ
አ፡ ቡ፡ ወ፡ ደ
ተ፡ ት፡ ክ፡ መ፡ ዘ

ለእመ፡ኢንየዐግም
ዎ፡እነ፡እፈንዋ፡ን
ቢ፡ከሙ፡ከሙ፡የ፩
ልቅሙ፡ወይ፡ቤል
ዎ፡ትክልነ፡ዋቲሲ
ቱ፡ወነእምን፡ን፡ሐ
ነ፡በእምሳክከ፡ወ
ይቢ፡እወ፡እክል
በ፡ሀይሰ፡እግዚእ፡የ
ኢየሱስ፡ክርስቶስ፡
ወዘንተ፡በሂ፡ሰዐ
ሐረ፡እፍአ፡እምህ
ገር፡መጠነ፡ዐምዐ
ራፍ፡ወተለ፡ውዋ፡
ሕዝብ፡ከመ፡ይር
አይዎ፡ዘይገብር፡
ወቅዱስ፡ጊዮርጊ
ስ፡ወረደ፡እምነ፡ፈ
ረሱ፡ወፈትሐ፡ቅና
ተ፡እምክሳየ፡ከይ

ሲ፡ወቀነተ፡ሐቊሁ፡
ወተዐዕነ፡ዲበ፡ፈረ
ሱ፡ወረገ፡ዘክዓጅ፡
ወሞተ፡ወሰበር
ዱ፡ዘንተ፡ተአምሬ
ዘገበረ፡እግዚእነ፡
ኢየሱስ፡ክርስቶስ
በእደ፡ገብሩ፡ቅዱስ
ጊዮርጊስ፡ኮከቡ ክ
ብር፡አምኑ፡ሶሶ
ሙ፡ሰብአ፡ቢሩት፡
ወመጽአ፡ዕጻህን፡
ወእጥመቆሙ፡በ
ስመ፡አብ፡ወወል
ድ፡ወመንፈስ፡ቅዱ
ስ፡ወተምህሩ፡መ
ጻሕፍተ፡ወቅዱ
ጊዮርጊስ፡አተወ፡
ብሔር፡ወእሙ
ንቱሂ፡ሐነጹ፡ሰ

ቱ፡በስመ፡ፀ አብያ
ተ፡ክርስቲያናት፡
፰በማዕከስ፡ቢተት
ወ፮ን፡ቡ፡ዘቀተሰ፡
ስራጎን፡ወዘሰ፡እ
ከነ፡ዮም፡ጾሎ፡ት፡
ወበረከቱ፡ለቅዱ
ስ፡ጊዮርጊስ፡የሀ
ሉ፡ምክስ፡ፍቁሩ
ጊዮርጊስ፡ወምክስ
ፍቅርቱ፡ዓመቱ፡
ላሴ፡ወውሉዱ፡ገ
ስ፡ጊዮርጊስ፡ስዳ
መ፡ዓለም፡አሜን

Handel's *Messiah*

George Frideric Handel's most famous oratorio, *Messiah*, was first performed in Dublin in 1743, and this is the score from which the composer himself conducted its first performance. The original composing score is in the British Library. For performance it was copied by Handel's principal copyist, John Christopher Smith, and then amended and annotated by the composer himself. Here, for the aria 'Rejoice, rejoice, rejoice greatly', the copyist has written out the base line and the composer has filled in a new (and now familiar) version of the vocal and violin lines above it. Handel himself also noted in pencil (still just visible) the names of those who sang it at various performances – in this case the soprano Giulia Frasi, a tenor named John Beard and an anonymous treble referred to simply as 'The Boy'.

This important manuscript belonged in the nineteenth century to the Heather professor of music at Oxford, Sir Frederick Gore Ouseley, and went with his outstanding collection to St Michael's College, Tenbury Wells, which he founded in 1856 to encourage the young in the study and performance of cathedral-style music and worship. Under the terms of his will his manuscripts, numbering over one thousand, passed to the Bodleian Library when the college closed in 1985.

MS. Tenbury 346, fol. 66r

Allegro Senza Rip:
66
pian
Re
joyce rejoyce rejoyce greatly rejoyce
pian

The unbuilt Radcliffe Camera

The Radcliffe Camera – perhaps the most photographed building in Oxford, and since 1862 part of the Bodleian Library (see p. 13) – was constructed between 1738 when the foundation stone was laid and 1749 when the reading room was officially opened. The architect originally selected by the trustees of the benefactor John Radcliffe was Nicholas Hawksmoor and they paid £87.11s. for a model from his design to be made by John Smallwell. The model, said to have been used as a doll's house for many years at Ditchley Park in Oxfordshire, was given to the Bodleian in 1913 and has recently been restored. Hawksmoor died in 1736 and the commission passed to James Gibbs, who considerably modified the design, keeping the circular form but altering the dome, the fenestration and the external embellishment, and replacing Hawksmoor's square base with a polygonal one.

Both the masons appointed to construct the building – Francis Smith of Warwick and William Townesend of Oxford – died within a year of work starting, and each was succeeded by his son. Before he died, however, Francis Smith, by then a man of considerable bulk, had his portrait painted (probably by Hamlet Winstanley, though a subsequent engraving ascribes it to William Winstanley). Smith sits with his dividers poised over the Hawksmoor plan while in the background stands

a building clearly based on Hawksmoor's model. It is an example of a portrait of an important builder taking pride in a building that was never built to the design depicted. The portrait was bought for the Bodleian by the Radcliffe Trustees in 1984.

When the Camera first opened as a library to Gibbs's design it was run by two men: the librarian and a liveried porter who carried this impressive staff. The silver bull's head crest tops John Radcliffe's coat of arms.

The Porter's Staff, Hawksmoor's model (Library object 616); Portrait of Smith of Warwick (LP 709)

An eighteenth-century book auction

In the mid-eighteenth century when this picture was painted, the practice of holding book auctions had spread from London to Oxford, where they were conducted principally by members of the Fletcher family. A member of this family, Alderman William Fletcher (1739–1826), founder of the Old Bank (now a hotel), three times mayor of Oxford, notable antiquary and a frequent benefactor of the Bodleian Library, lived at 46 Broad Street and this picture by William Green Jr was said to be hanging in the 1880s in the front room of that house. The house was one of those demolished in 1937 to make way for the building of the New Bodleian (now the Weston) Library. The picture was presented to the Bodleian by the executors of John Bryson (b. 1896) fellow of Balliol College in 1980.

In a room lined with shelves from floor to ceiling an auction is in progress. Some thirty-five persons, all male, are present, taking down, examining or discussing the volumes being sold. All save one are in academic dress. The exception, smartly attired in a striking yellow coat, is one of the few people taking any notice of the auctioneer. The occasion depicted is not made clear – perhaps the sale of a particular library, the arrival in the sale room of a distinguished visitor or even a particular purchase.

LP 701

178

179

Yankee Doodle

This seemingly ordinary English song sheet is a great rarity. It is one of the thousands of such rarities that came to the Bodleian Library in its biggest ever donation: the twenty-two tonnes of rare books, sheet music, opera scores and printed ephemera amassed in Chicago by Walter N. Harding (1883–1973). London-born, he moved to Chicago at the age of 4 and became a music hall pianist and cinema organist while putting together the formidable musical collection that now bears his name. The collection arrived at the Bodleian in 1975, two years after his death.

Yankee Doodle is now thought of as a quintessentially American song, but this song sheet, the earliest known edition to carry the music, is English. Published by Thomas Skillern (the 'Sk:' at the foot of the sheet), a prolific music publisher, it is one of only three copies known to exist and the only one in the UK. The origins of the song are far from clear. It was said to have been sung as a marching song by British troops in North America satirizing their colonial counterparts during the French and Indian War (1754–68). The instruction 'The Words to be Sung thro' the Nose, & in the West Country drawl & dialect' may indicate an attempt to imitate the colonial accent. The words in this version are scurrilous. The 'Brother Ephraim' of the opening verse is taken to be a reference to Ephraim Williams Jr (1715–55), the founder of Williams College, Mass., who, as colonel in the Massachusetts Militia was killed in an ambush on the road between Lake George and Fort Edward on 8 September 1755.

When the American War of Independence broke out, British troops sang the song as they marched into battle in the first military engagement at Lexington, Mass., on 19 April 1775, mocking their opponents as Yankee 'doodles' or yokels. Almost immediately, however, it was adopted as a popular marching song by colonial troops and has remained (with changed words) as an American patriotic anthem ever since.

The sheet is undated, but the reference to Lexington puts it after 1775. It is one of five thousand or so song sheets in the Harding collection.

Harding Mus. G. 70 (3)

YANKEE DOODLE, or
(as now Christened by the SAINTS of New England)
THE LEXINGTON MARCH

NB. The Words to be Sung thrô the Nose, & in the West Country drawl & dialect.

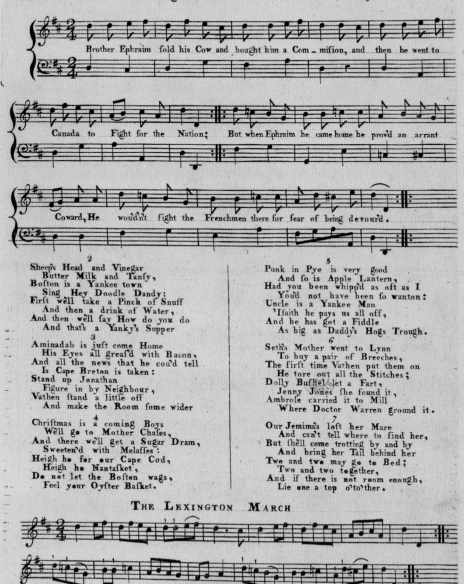

Brother Ephraim fold his Cow and bought him a Com___mifion, and then he went to Canada to Fight for the Nation; But when Ephraim he came home he prov'd an arrant Coward, He woudn't fight the Frenchmen there for fear of being devourd.

2
Sheeps Head and Vinegar
    Butter Milk and Tanfy,
Bofton is a Yankee town
    Sing Hey Doodle Dandy:
First we'll take a Pinch of Snuff
    And then a drink of Water,
And then we'll fay How do you do
    And that's a Yanky's Supper

3
Aminadab is juft come Home
    His Eyes all greas'd with Bacon,
And all the news that he cou'd tell
    Is Cape Breton is taken:
Stand up Jonathan
    Figure in by Neighbour,
Vathen ftand a little off
    And make the Room fome wider

4
Chriftmas is a coming Boys
    We'll go to Mother Chafes,
And there we'll get a Sugar Dram,
    Sweeten'd with Melaffes:
Heigh ho for our Cape Cod,
    Heigh ho Nantafket,
Do not let the Bofton wags,
    Feel your Oyfter Bafket.

5
Punk in Pye is very good
    And fo is Apple Lantern,
Had you been whipp'd as oft as I
    You'd not have been fo wanton:
Uncle is a Yankee Man
    'Ifaith he pays us all off,
And he has got a Fiddle
    As big as Daddy's Hogs Trough.

6
Seth's Mother went to Lynn
    To buy a pair of Breeches,
The firft time Vathen put them on
    He tore out all the Stitches;
Dolly Buffiel let a Fart,
    Jenny Jones fhe found it,
Ambrofe carried it to Mill
    Where Doctor Warren ground it.

7
Our Jemima's loft her Mare
    And can't tell where to find her,
But fhe'll come trotting by and by
    And bring her Tail behind her
Two and two may go to Bed;
    Two and two together,
And if there is not room enough,
    Lie one a top o'to'ther.

THE LEXINGTON MARCH

Sk:

A Chinese Emperor's poems

This exquisite small Chinese book contains twenty poems by the Emperor Gaozong, who ruled from 1736 to 1796. The poems are in the hand of the grand secretary and scholar Liu Lun (1711–73). Measuring a mere 95 x 50 x 15mm, it is constructed so that it unfolds like the bellows of an accordion and its outer covers are of jade. Its endpapers are decorated with cloud patterns in gold dust. The jade cover is engraved with the title and authorship details. It is the only jade binding in the Bodleian Library.

It came as one among some 27,000 volumes collected in China and given to the Bodleian between 1913 and 1922 by Sir Edmund Trelawny Backhouse, Bart. (1873–1944). He was referred to in 1952 in Sir Edmund Craster's *History of the Bodleian Library, 1845–1945* as 'a gentleman long resident in Pekin' and 'a scholar of repute'. However, his bizarre life story was chronicled in detail by Hugh Trevor-Roper in *A Hidden Life: the Enigma of Sir Edmund Backhouse* (1976), so that he is now characterized in The Oxford Dictionary of National Biography as a 'Sinologist and fraudster' who 'was throughout his life hermitic, eccentric, evasive, litigious, profligate, and a gross snob; but he was also charmingly gentlemanly and persuasive'.

He was certainly a great benefactor of the Library, his gifts instituting what was probably at the time the finest collection of Chinese books outside the far east. He had declined the offer of a chair in Chinese at King's College in London, in the expectation that he would be offered that at Oxford. When his hopes were dashed he ceased to add to the collection, though financed to do so by the Bodleian. In his notoriously unreliable (indeed often fanciful) memoirs, *Décadence mandchoue*, Backhouse describes receiving on 26 June 1902 a book bound in jade and containing poems by Liu Lun as a gift from the then grand secretary Ronglu, but whether it is this one cannot now be known.

MS. Backhouse 11 (Arch O f.12)

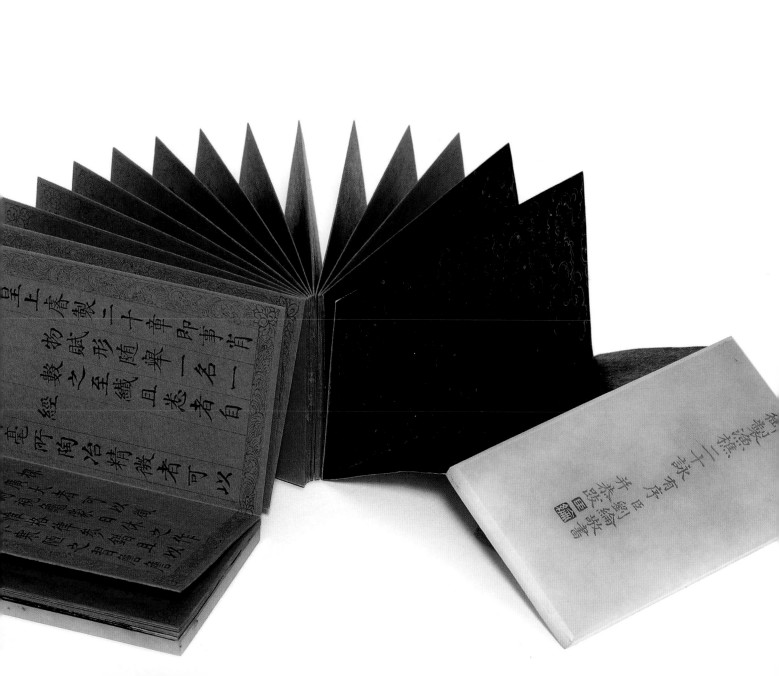

The Persian New Testament

This beautiful example of Persian book art stands as a memorial to a remarkable man: the Rev. Henry Martyn (1781–1812). A Cornish boy who was an accomplished classical linguist, he went to Cambridge University at the age of 16, where he excelled as a mathematician. He was destined for a legal career but, influenced by the missionary work of the Baptist William Carey (1761–1834), he took holy orders and sailed to India as a chaplain to the British East India Company in 1806 at the age of 25. There during the following six years he employed his linguistic talents in translating the New Testament into the three main Islamic languages: Arabic, Urdu and Persian. Though in poor health, he travelled to Persia in order to complete his work and personally to present the Shah with a copy of the Persian translation which he completed in 1812. His health broke down completely, however, and on his way back to England he died of tuberculosis at Tokat in Anatolia in October 1812, aged 31. A copy was eventually presented to the Shah by the British ambassador, Sir Gore Ouseley.

This stunning copy made in Shiraz in south-western Iran where Martyn was working in 1812 seems also to have been intended as a presentation copy. The highly decorated opening is the beginning of the gospel of Matthew, with its title in gold and the text in blue, red and black in Nasta'līq script. The volume is clad in a fine Qajar floral lacquer binding.

It came to the Bodleian Library as one of the collection of over four hundred volumes given in 1859 by J.B. Elliott of Patra, of which many had been originally collected by Sir Gore Ouseley during his diplomatic service in the east.

MS. Elliott 14, binding, and fols. 1v – 2r

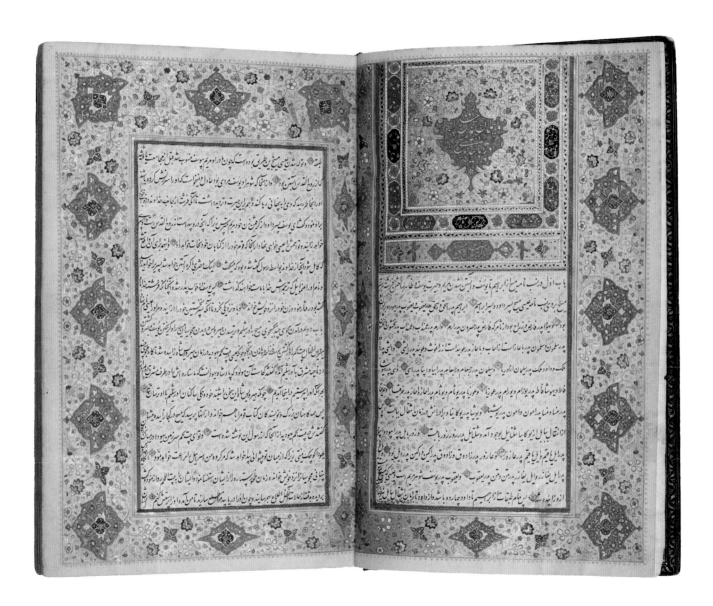

The Buddha in a past life

Books take many shapes. This fine example of Siamese art and craftsmanship in book form originated in the eighteenth century in what is now Thailand. It was produced as an aid for monks in a Buddhist temple as they chanted stories describing the Bodhisatta – the journey through many different lives of the Buddha before his last incarnation. Made from mulberry paper and known as a samut khoi, its width and slim profile derived from earlier manuscripts made from palm leaf or birch bark – materials whose very nature dictated the shape of the resulting book. Paper made from pulped mulberry leaves may be produced in a variety of shapes, but the traditional form led to sheets being glued end to end and then folded within a lacquered cover to be stored in concertina fashion and then unfolded and read as their predecessors had been. The text is in *Pāli* and written in Khom script. The accompanying pictures do not necessarily relate, as in the western tradition, to the text alongside them, both script and pictures being texts acting as prompts to a temple chanter as he expounded the story of the Bodhisatta's path to Buddhahood. The folded manuscript is 660mm wide and 95mm deep.

As photographed here, it is unfolded to show two paintings illustrating the *Temiya-Jātaka* or the life of the Bodhisatta as Prince Temiya and his acquisition of one of the ten perfections – that of renunciation. Temiya as a small child renounced the kingship which was to be his inheritance by pretending to be deaf, mute, and incapacitated, maintaining the pretence for sixteen years despite all attempts to provoke him. In the picture on the viewer's right he is shown remaining passive despite the blandishments of scantily clad young women, while that on the left shows how, when threatened with death, he emerged from his long soundless and motionless state, dancing and lifting a chariot over his head. His renunciation of his kingdom stood, however, and he became a hermit.

The manuscript, perhaps the finest of its kind to survive, was almost certainly commissioned in Siam (now Thailand) in the second half of the eighteenth century to be sent to Ceylon (now Sri Lanka) as part of a movement to revitalize Buddhism there. It was subsequently acquired there by the collector and port attendant William Carmichael Gibson (1768–1832), from whom it passed to the Gibson-Craig family, whose estate was sold in 1888. Bought by the dealer Bernard Quaritch, it was then acquired by the Bodleian Library.

MS. Pali a. 27 (R), fol. 6

187

A relic of an attempted assassination

This playbill for the performance of two plays at the Theatre Royal, Drury Lane, London, on 15 May 1800 is no ordinary one. It is printed on silk and was being carried by King George III when he went to the front of the royal box in the theatre to acknowledge the playing of the National Anthem. At that moment, from the pit, an ex-soldier named James Hadfield fired two shots at the king with a horse pistol. It was the second time that day that an apparent attempt had been made on the king's life. Earlier, during a review of the Grenadiers in Hyde Park, a musket ball had wounded a spectator some 23 feet (7m) away from the king. Once again, in the evening the king was unharmed but in the ensuing melee this playbill was dropped. It was gathered up by a person unknown and subsequently presented to Lord Amherst. It is now in the John Johnson Collection of Printed Ephemera in the Bodleian Library.

The would-be regicide James Hadfield was quickly overpowered. A 29-year-old, he had suffered severe sabre wounds to the head and had been captured by the French while serving under the Duke of York at the Battle of Tourcoing in Flanders in May 1794. He had come to believe that the second coming of Jesus Christ depended on his own death at the hands of the British government, and in order to achieve this he resolved to kill the king – against whom he had no personal animosity. Indeed, he is reported to have subsequently said to King George: 'God bless your royal highness; I like you very well; you are a good fellow.' Charged with high treason, he was defended by Thomas Erskine and was acquitted in a case which altered British society's view on the criminal responsibility of those deemed insane or partially insane. He spent the remaining forty-one years of his life in the Bethlehem Royal Hospital (Bedlam).

John Johnson Collection: Playbills on Silk (11a)

THEATRE ROYAL,
DRURY LANE.

THEIR MAJESTIES.

This present THURSDAY, MAY 15th. 1800,
THEIR MAJESTIES SERVANTS will perform a COMEDY called

She Wou'd & She Wou'd Not;
Or, The Kind Impostor.

Don Manuel, Mr. KING,
Don Philip, Mr. BARRYMORE,
Octavio, Mr. HOLLAND,
Trappanti, Mr. BANNISTER, Jun.
Soto, Mr. WATHEN,
Don Lewis, Mr. SURMONT,
Diego, Mr. HOLLINGSWORTH.

Hippolita, Mrs. JORDAN,
Rosara, Miss HEARD,
Flora, Miss DE CAMP,
Viletta, Miss POPE.

To which (BY COMMAND) will be added the FARCE of The

HUMOURIST.

Sir Anthony Halfwit, Mr. SUETT,
Dabble, Mr BANNISTER, Jun.
Frolick, Mr. HOLLINGSWORTH,
Beaumont, Mr. CAULFIELD,
Servants, Mr. FISHER, Mr. EVANS,
Blunt, Mr. WEBB.

Mrs. Matadore, Mrs. WALCOT,
Diana, Miss HEARD,
Mrs. Meddle, Miss TIDSWELL.

Printed by C. Lowndes, Drury-Lane.

VIVANT REX ET REGINA.

The Bill which the King
had in his hand when he
was shot at on the 15th of May 1800

Pictorial patriotism

France declared war on Britain in February 1793, and from then until the French fleet was defeated at the Battle of Trafalgar in October 1805 – save for a period of uneasy peace in 1802 and 1803 – Britain felt constantly under threat of invasion by Napoleon's army. The threat generated a mass of patriotic pamphlets, cartoons and caricatures in which Bonaparte, his army and his fleet are depicted confronting a determined foe symbolized by a gruff, rotund John Bull.

A great collection of these ephemeral items was made by Alexander Meyrick Broadley (1847–1916). Some 1,200 cartoons and caricatures from his collections were bought at the sale of his library in 1916 by the Marquess Curzon of Kedleston (1859–1925), chancellor of the University of Oxford, to which he bequeathed them along with a collection of Napoleonic furniture and memorabilia.

This one is by James Gillray (1726–1815), who as the foremost political caricaturist of the late eighteenth century established an art form which flourishes to this day. Published by Hannah Humphrey on 10 June 1803, it purports to show a small force of British artillery under the Union Flag routing a huge French invasion force with Napoleon himself, on a white charger, hatless and, having thrown away his sabre, caught up in the headlong flight.

Curzon b.22 (62)

190

FRENCH INVASION or BUONAPARTE

Publish'd June 18th 1803 by H Humphrey 27 St James's Street — London

Jane Austen

No original manuscript survives for any of the six novels on which the fame of Jane Austen (1775–1817), perhaps the most celebrated of all female writers in English, rests. However, preserved in the Bodleian Library are two manuscripts in her hand that show first the budding writer as a child and later the accomplished novelist at work.

The first, acquired and given to the library by the Friends of the Bodleian in 1933, shows Jane, the young daughter of a well-to-do country parson, between the ages of 12 and 15, writing amusing stories for the entertainment of her family. Later, aged 18 in 1793, she copied the stories out into three small notebooks of which this one, entitled 'Volume the first', is the earliest. 'Volume the second' and 'Volume the third' are in the British Library.

Volume the first contains fourteen stories or other pieces. Illustrated here is the start of 'Jack & Alice, a novel' in which the young Jane's satirical humour is already in evidence in the opening sentence. Dedicated to her favourite brother, Francis, who later rose to the rank of admiral in the Royal Navy, the text was not published until 1933, when an edition was produced by R.W. Chapman, through whom the manuscript came to the Bodleian.

In contrast to this finished juvenile short novel, the second manuscript illustrated here, acquired by the Bodleian in 2011, consists of sixty-eight pages of closely written and heavily corrected and revised text for a novel that the mature Jane never completed. Probably written in 1804–05, it is an unnamed draft, material from which was used by Jane in *Mansfield Park* and later by her niece Catherine Hubback (daughter of Jane's brother Francis) in her first novel *The Younger Sister* in 1850. It was eventually published in 1871 under the title *The Watsons* by a nephew of Jane's sister Cassandra, James Edward Austen-Leigh. The manuscript now lacks its first six leaves, which were removed and given to a First World War charity sale in 1915 by a later member of the Austen-Leigh family. They are now in the Pierpont Morgan Library in New York.

The two manuscripts also show how the monetary value put upon such literary papers changed during the second half of the twentieth century. In 1933 *Volume the first* was acquired by the Friends of the Bodleian for £75. In 2011 the manuscript of *The Watsons* realized £1,072,900 in the saleroom and its acquisition was made possible only with substantial aid from the Heritage Lottery Fund, the Friends of the National Libraries, the Friends of the Bodleian and many other benefactors.

MS. Don. e. 7, pp. 22–23; MS. Eng. e. 3764

the Trouble of at ...

was an old grievance ... "So late, my dear, returned ...
saw you talking of," cried the husband with
pleasantry. "we are always at home before
midnight. They would laugh at Osborne Castle
to hear you call that late; they are but just
rising from dinner at midnight." "That is
nothing to the purpose," retorted the Lady.
"The Osbornes are to be no rule for us. You
had meet every night & break up two
hours sooner." so far, the subject was very
often carried; but Mr & Mrs Edwards were curious
... never to pass that point, & Mrs Edwards
... nothing else, the had lived ...
... the Idleness of a Town ...

Jack & Alice
a novel.
respectfully inscribed to Francis William Austen
Esqr. Midshipman on board his Majesty's Ship the Perseverance by his obedient humble Servant The Author
Chapter the first

Mr Johnson was once upon a time about
53; in a twelvemonth afterwards he was
54, which so much delighted him that he
was determined to celebrate his next
birth day by giving a Masquerade to his
Children & Freinds. Accordingly on the
Day he attained his 55th year tickets
were dispatched to all his Neighbours
to that purpose. His acquaintance indeed
in that part of the World were not very
numerous as they consisted only of Lady

Williams, Mr & Mrs Jones, Charles Adams
& the 3 Miss Simpsons, who composed
the neighbourhood of Pammydiddle &
formed the Masquerade.
Before I proceed to give an account
of the Evening, it will be proper to
describe to my readers, the persons and
Characters of the party introduced to his acquaintance.
Mr & Mrs Jones' were both rather tall
& very passionate, but were in other
respects, good tempered, well behaved Peo:
:ple. Charles Adams was an amiable,
accomplished & bewitching young Man;
of so dazzling a Beauty that none
but Eagles could look him in the Face.
Miss Simpson was pleasing in
her person, in her Manners & in her Disposi:
:tion;

An American hero and a British schoolboy

In 1813, when an 8-year-old schoolboy at Warrington in the north of England sought to impress his elders with his handwriting, Britain was at war with the United States of America, yet the paper on which he wrote was decorated with scenes from the life of an American hero, Benjamin Franklin.

Franklin (1706–1790) had been one of the leading figures in the break from Great Britain that followed a previous war with the motherland: the American Revolutionary War. He had been dead for twenty-three years when young Thomas Hatton wrote his letter, but one can see why the publishers of the single-sheet Writing Blank (or School Piece) should consider that his life would serve as a good model for the young in early nineteenth-century England. In the primitive but attractively coloured engravings Franklin is depicted being led by his father to be bound apprentice to his brother, a printer in Boston; labouring at delivering newspapers; and leaving Boston for Philadelphia, where he joins the Quakers, meets his wife – a printer's daughter – works hard to open his own shop and

cultivates an enquiring scientific mind. The final two engravings show him as ambassador in Paris negotiating peace with Great Britain and becoming president of the province of Pennsylvania.

This Writing Blank, printed in 1808 by W. & T. Darton, is one in a folder of such blanks in the enormous collection of ephemeral printing begun by John Johnson (1882–1956), printer to the university. It was transferred from Oxford University Press to the Bodleian Library in 1968. In showing off his handwriting skills, the young Thomas Hatton was perhaps employing the enterprise of Franklin in not only seeking to impress his aunt or uncle but also seeking a subsidy from them.

On the previous blank in the folder another young scholar penned the adult thinking behind these exercises:

He most improves who studies with delight
And learns sound morals whilst he learns to write

John Johnson Collection Educational Folder 5 (21a)

194

ADVENTURES of FRANKLIN.

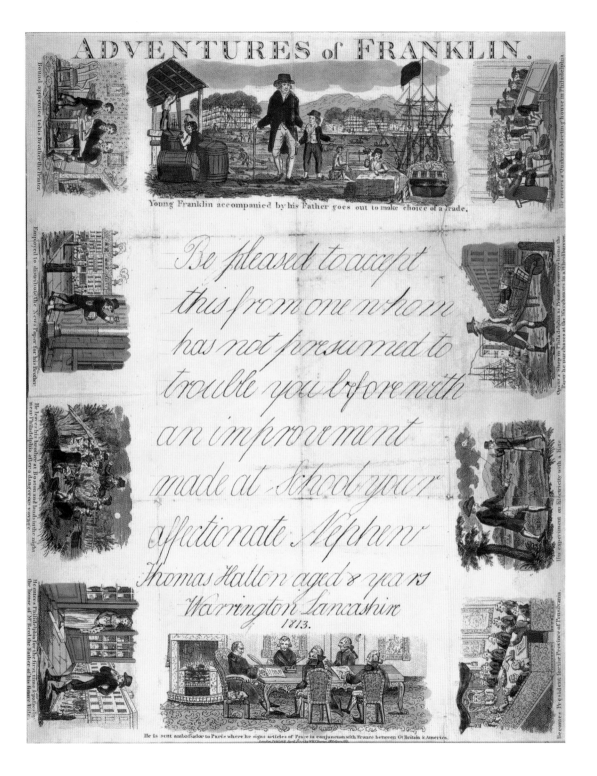

Young Franklin accompanied by his Father goes out to make choice of a Trade.

Bound apprentice to his Brother the Printer.

He enters a Quakers Meeting house in Philadelphia.

Employed to distribute the News Paper for his brother.

Opens a Shop in Philadelphia as Printer & carrys home the Paper he purchases at the Warehouses in a Wheelbarrow.

He leaves his brother at Boston and finds in the night near Philadelphia after a dangerous voyage.

His experiment on Electricity with a Kite.

He enters Philadelphia for the first time & places the house of Mr Read the Father of his future Wife.

Be pleased to accept this from one whom has not presumed to trouble you before with an improvement made at School your affectionate Nephew

Thomas Halton aged 8 years
Warrington Lancashire
1813.

He is sent ambassador to Paris where he signs articles of Peace in conjunction with France between Gt Britain & America.

Becomes President for the Province of Pensilvania.

Shelley relics

The turbulent life of the Romantic poet Percy Bysshe Shelley and his death by drowning at the age of 29 in 1822 have been written about again and again. Given that he had departed from Oxford in 1811 under a cloud, having been sent down from University College, it is perhaps remarkable that his descendants in the late nineteenth and twentieth centuries presented to the Bodleian many of his notebooks and other items associated with him. Subsequently the library has acquired more by purchase. Illustrated here is the page in one of his notebooks on which the 'Ode to the West Wind' may be seen in the process of composition some three years before his death, 'in a wood that skirts the Arno, near Florence' as he subsequently wrote, 'and on a day when that tempestuous wind, whose temperature is at once mild and animating, was collecting the vapours which pour down the autumnal rains'.

Shelley's relationship with his father, Sir Timothy Shelley, had broken down many years before the poet's death in 1822, and until his own death in 1844 Sir Timothy forbade the poet's four sisters from even mentioning his name. Later, the poet's son and daughter-in-law worked to achieve reconciliation within the family – a reconciliation symbolized in this portrait of the poet's sisters Hellen and Margaret. Margaret, the younger sister, who is standing, wears a necklace made from the hair of Mary Wollstonecraft, the feminist mother of Mary Shelley, with whom the poet had eloped in 1814. Attached to the necklace are two lockets containing the hair of the poet and his wife. The necklace itself (pictured above) is also in the Bodleian collection.

MS. Shelley adds. e. 12, p. 63; Shelley relics 8 (opposite) and (1) (above)

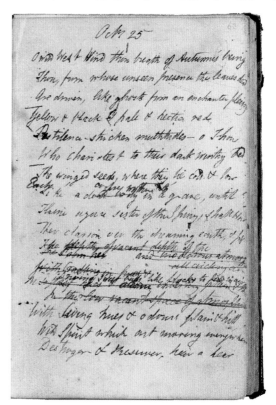

Mendelssohn's *Hebrides* Overture

The Bodleian Library and the Staatsbibliothek in Berlin
are the two principal centres for research into the
life and music of the composer Felix Mendelssohn
Bartholdy. The Bodleian's collection came principally
by donation from descendants of the composer
between 1960 and 1974, and is particularly strong on
biographical material, student notes, diaries, albums,
drawings, letters received by the composer and much
of his musical library. The Bodleian has subsequently
made additions to this collection by purchase, and
in 2002, the 400th anniversary year of its opening –

aided by its Friends and by the Heritage Lottery Fund
– it acquired at auction Mendelssohn's final working
manuscript of perhaps his best-known overture, *Hebrides*
or *Fingal's Cave*. Inspired by a visit to Scotland in 1829,
the piece took almost three years to reach this final
version, itself full of revisions and dated London,
20 June 1832. Five years later he gave it to his friend
William Sterndale Bennett, in whose family it remained
until acquired by the Bodleian.

MS. M. Deneke Mendelssohn d. 71, fol. 13r

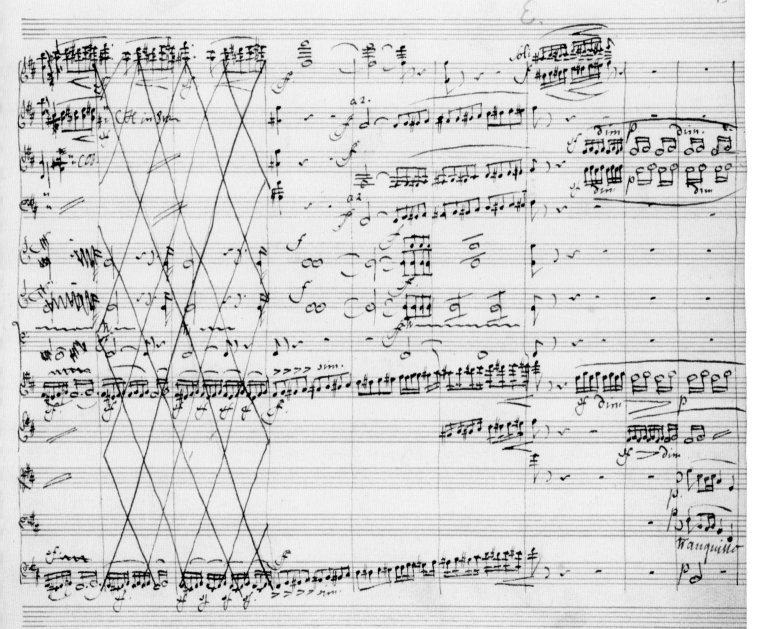

Julia Margaret Cameron and G.F. Watts

These two albumen prints by the great Victorian photographer Julia Margaret Cameron (1815–1879) are in an album containing 112 such prints that she gave to the eminent literary figure Sir Henry Taylor (1800–1886). The album was presented to the Bodleian Library in 1930 by the Taylor family, along with an archive of Sir Henry's correspondence, letter-books and diaries. While many of the prints depict Sir Henry himself, others are of members of the circle of literary and artistic figures who lived close to Cameron on the Isle of Wight or who visited regularly in the 1860s, including Alfred, Lord Tennyson, Thomas Carlyle, Benjamin Jowett, Robert Browning, William Holman Hunt, Ellen Terry, William Michael Rossetti and Sir John Herschel – who had introduced her to the techniques and possibilities of the science of photography earlier in the century.

During the 1860s Cameron became absorbed by the challenges presented by the camera, and in her photographs of individuals strove to emulate the best portrait painters in not simply producing flattering likenesses but trying, as she herself said of her portraits of Thomas Carlyle, to capture faithfully 'the greatness of the inner as well as the features of the outer man'. Her use of natural light and therefore long exposures required her sitters to remain still and with their eyes open for lengthy periods, investing the resultant portraits with a great intensity.

The two portraits reproduced here are of a man who became a famous – perhaps the most famous – portrait painter of the day: George Frederick Watts (1817–1904). They are markedly different from one another, that on the left appearing much closer to the image conveyed in his self-portraits. It is not known which of them was thought by contemporaries to convey better the greatness of the inner man.

Arch. K b.12, fols. 71r and 72r

Two eminent Victorians

This photograph was taken in 1893 by Sarah Angelina Acland. It portrays her father, Sir Henry Wentworth Dyke Acland, the eminent physician who was regius professor of medicine at Oxford from 1858 to 1894, showing one of his sketchbooks to John Ruskin during a visit to Ruskin's house at Brantwood in Cumbria. Ruskin had been a frequent visitor to the Acland family home in Broad Street, Oxford, which was demolished in the 1930s during the building of the New Bodleian (now the Weston) Library. In 1930, in her eighty-first year, Miss Acland, an accomplished portrait photographer, compiled a volume of prints of photographs taken between 1891 and 1900 of eminent persons who had visited the Aclands in Broad Street. She then annotated them and, handsomely bound, they were presented to the Friends of the Bodleian. Her memories of Ruskin, the art critic and social reformer, were fond ones. She called him, somewhat strangely, 'The Fairy Godmother of our childhood', remembering in particular a doll given to her by the great man and dressed by his wife. She recalled too 'the most amusing scenes taking place [between Ruskin and Acland] especially when trying to play whist which neither of them knew'.

MS. Don. d. 14, fol. 23r

Two future kings

In 1906 and 1908 respectively, two 12-year-old brothers were entered for cadetships at the Royal Naval College at Osborne. They were Edward and Albert, grandsons of the king of England, Edward VII – the sons of George, duke of York, who was to succeed his father in 1910 as George V. These two young boys were themselves both subsequently to become kings; Edward as Edward VIII in 1936 and, following his abdication later that year, Albert as George VI. Neither boy had ever been to school. They had been privately tutored, principally by H.P. Hansell, who submitted a report on them to the first lord of the Admiralty together with a sample of their written work. The photograph of them with their mother is in the Royal Collection.

Illustrated are the essays that each wrote in his own hand. Prince Edward's subject was Henry VIII who 'took part in foreign wars, generally against France'. His wives are all listed and reference made to his most famous ship (apparently inspired by the boy's having seen it depicted on a calendar). Prince Albert wrote about his 'favourite amusement' which was football and in which he played at 'left half-back'. He had 'played in several matches and won nearly all of them'.

The contrast between the handwriting is striking. Hansell in his report on Prince Edward highlighted his sense of humour, his excellent ear for music and his fine physique, but pointed out a 'tendency to be disheartened'. His weak point was 'orthography. He has great difficulty in spelling' – evidenced here in the names of Henry VIII's wives. Prince Albert, however, whose handwriting perhaps displays the fact that though naturally left-handed he was made to write with his right hand, was characterized by Hansell as 'scatter-brained' with 'a nervous habit of speech which the doctors say will disappear as he develops'. His weakness was therefore in 'viva voce work' but he had a gift for sports, particularly for golf, at which 'he plays a beautiful game'.

The essays together with the reports were retained by Sir Vincent Baddeley, the private secretary to the first lord of the Admiralty. He presented them to the Bodleian in 1953.

MS. Eng. misc. c. 868, fols. 1r and 3r

204

Henry VIII.
1509 – 1547.

Henry took part in foreign wars, generally against France.

At first he upheld the Roman Catholick religion and received title of Defendor of the Faith for writing a book against Luther, but the divorce of Catherine of Aragon led to fall of Wolsey and Reformation.

Henry had six wives i. e. Catherine of Aragon, Ann Boulein, Jane Seymoure, & Ann of Cleives, Catherine Howard, and Catherine Parr. Henry visited Francis I of France on Field of Cloth of Gold. He carried out Dissolution of

My favourite amusement is football. I like it because I have played a good a deal of it. My place is left half-back. I have played in several matches and won nearly all of them. The benefits of the game are that it is a quick game and a good game for winter in which season it is played. It is very exciting when the ball is near the goal. At all nearly every match there are hundreds of people who enjoy it. It is a very manly game, because the players do not really mind if they are hurt or not.

It is a good test to see if the players are up to the game.

PUBLISHED AT THE
WINTER QUARTERS
OF THE BRITISH
ANTARCTIC EXPED
ITION, 1907, DURING
THE WINTER MON
THS OF APRIL, MAY,
JUNE, JULY, 1908.
ILLUSTRATED WITH
LITHOGRAPHS AND
ETCHINGS; BY
GEORGE MARSTON

PRINTED AT THE SIGN OF
'THE PENGUINS'; BY JOYCE
AND WILD.
LATITUDE 77°·· 32' SOUTH
LONGITUDE 166°·· 12' EAST
ANTARCTICA

TRADE MARK

Ernest Shackleton's Antarctic Press

When Ernest Shackleton set out with the British Antarctic Nimrod Expedition of 1907–09, perhaps the most surprising of all the items of equipment accompanying him were an Albion printing press, an etching press, types, inks (in three colours) and paper. His intention was, during the dark Antarctic winter, to encourage members of his team to write, illustrate, print and bind one hundred copies of a book. To this end he had persuaded the printing firm Sir Joseph Causton & Sons Ltd to give him the equipment and to give two of his men, Ernest Joyce and Frank Wild, along with the expedition's artist George Marston, three weeks' training. Once on the ice he set up a printing office measuring a mere 6 by 7 feet (1.8 x 2.13m) which accommodated not only the machinery (and a large sewing machine) but also bunks for two men.

This extraordinary effort resulted during the cold and dark winter months in the production of *Aurora Australis. Published at the winter quarters of the British Antarctic Expedition, 1907, during the winter months of April, May, June, July, 1908. Illustrated with lithographs and etchings; by George Marston.* It contains prose and verse contributions from members of the expedition about their life in the Antarctic, with a preface by Shackleton himself. The text, printed on 108 individual leaves, was bound by Bernard Day, who used wood from packing cases for the boards and sheepskin for the spine. It is signed by Shackleton and Marston.

This copy was acquired by the collector Albert Ehrman who, with his wife, formed the Broxbourne Library at their home in Hertfordshire, one of the specialities of which was a collection of books produced in 'out-of-the-way' places. Ehrman called the book 'the most interesting of my modern imprints'. The Broxbourne Library of early and fine printing, bindings and catalogues of printers, publishers, booksellers, auctioneers and libraries was presented to the Bodleian Library by Albert's son John Ehrman through the Friends of the National Libraries in 1978.

Broxb. 51.14, binding and title page

Casualties of war

The Bodleian Library houses many books whose importance lies not in their content but in their context. The two books illustrated here were presented to the library as casualties of two wars. While neither might deserve to be called a 'treasure', both survived significant battles and bear the scars.

The battered copy of Charles Dickens' *The Posthumous Papers of the Pickwick Club* in a Russian translation of c.1847 is a victim of the siege of Sevastopol during the Crimean War. That bloody eleven-month siege ended on 11 September 1856. Two days earlier, when one of its principal fortifications, the Redan, fell to the British, F.J. Holt Beever of Jesus College, Oxford, found there this book – presumably the reading material of one of the Russian defenders. On his return following the siege, during which over ten thousand men died, Mr Holt Beever gave it to the Bodleian.

The severely damaged copy of Edward Thomas's *Oxford* with illustrations by John Fulleylove was a casualty some sixty years later of the largest naval battle of the First World War, the Battle of Jutland, between the British Grand Fleet and the German navy's High Seas Fleet on 31 May and 1 June 1916. An accompanying letter from a chaplain in the Royal Navy, the Rev. Walter J. Carey of Hertford College, written in January 1918, says that during the battle he had a shell through his cabin in HMS *Warspite* and the book was damaged by sea-water. He placed it in the Bodleian 'as a relic for future ages'.

Arch. BB d.6; Arch. AA d.16

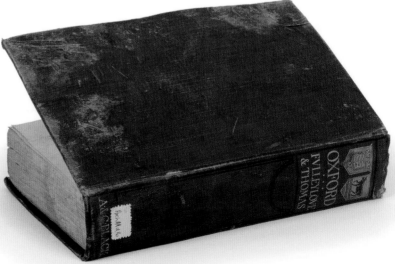

George VI's broken key

By the end of the first quarter of the twentieth century the Bodleian Library had run out of expansion space. A plan for a new large building close to its historic complex was drawn up. By 1929 a site had been acquired on the corner of Broad Street and Parks Road; in 1934 an architect, Sir Giles Gilbert Scott, was appointed; building work started late in 1936; and by 1940 it was virtually complete. Styled simply the New Library, its incorporation into the Bodleian was postponed by the Second World War, during which the huge new structure was used for other purposes. It was not formally opened until 24 October 1946 – some eighteen months after the war in Europe had ended. During the years 2012–14 the building was remodelled internally to reopen in 2015 as the Weston Library.

The ceremony at which it was originally opened by King George VI is now part of Oxford folklore. The

king, following the presentation of a loyal address in the Sheldonian Theatre, was given a 'beautifully designed' silver key with which to open the building, but when he inserted it in the lock the handle broke away from the shank, leaving the key stuck in the lock. The door could not be opened by those waiting inside and disaster was only averted when a strong-fingered Bedel of Arts managed to grip the shank and turn it. The key, pictured here, was presented to the king as a memento of the occasion, but he subsequently returned it with a letter asking that it should be placed 'among the historic relics preserved in the Library'.

Johnson d.3518; MS. Autogr. c. 16, fol. 24; Cons. Res. Objects 63

BODLEIAN LIBRARY
THE OPENING
OF THE
NEW LIBRARY
BY
HIS MAJESTY
KING GEORGE VI
24th OCTOBER 1946

BUCKINGHAM PALACE

This key, which broke in the lock when I attempted to open the door of the New Library at Oxford on October 24th 1946, was given by me to Bodley's Librarian on that day to be placed among the historic relics preserved in the Library.

George R.I.

J.R.R. Tolkien

J.R.R. Tolkien's international reputation rests on his pre-eminence in two fields: as a philological scholar, first at Leeds University and then successively as Rawlinson and Bosworth professor of Anglo-Saxon and Merton professor of English at Oxford; and as the author of the phenomenally popular stories *The Hobbit* (first published in 1937) and its successor *The Lord of the Rings* (first published in 1954–55).

However, from his earliest days, encouraged by his mother, he kept sketchbooks and learned from her a distinctive style of writing and drawing. By his teenage years he had become an accomplished artist in both watercolours and pen-and-ink and was fascinated by calligraphy. These skills he often used in later life to design illustrations and dust jackets for his works of fiction. He also used them in the years from 1920 to 1943 to write and illustrate Christmas letters to his four children. These were penned in a shaky hand and purported to be from Father Christmas himself. They came in decorated envelopes bearing polar stamps seemingly franked at the North Pole.

Two of them are illustrated here. The first letter, of 1920, written to his son John shows Father Christmas and his round house at the North Pole. The second, that of 1932, shows Father Christmas looking for his lost chief assistant, the North Polar Bear, in caves below the pole where the bear had strayed by mistake. In the caves are goblins, and 'Goblins', the letter explains, 'are to us very much what rats are to you, only worse because they are very clever, & only better because there are, in these parts, very few'. The caves were very dark and only when Father Christmas lit his torch were the walls shown to be covered in drawings made centuries earlier by cavemen who had lived in them. Above this picture is a second scene of Father Christmas's arrival from the north over the Tolkien house in Oxford on Christmas Eve. The letter explains the number of reindeer he preferred to use.

The letters were presented to the Bodleian Library along with many other Tolkien manuscripts and drawings by the Tolkien Trust in 1979 and 1984.

MSS. Tolkien drawings 38 and 57

FROM FATHER · CHRISTMAS

ME

FC

MY HOUSE

FC

1932

A merry christmas

NC

C.S. Lewis's map of Narnia

The first of C.S. Lewis's seven Narnia stories, *The Lion, the Witch and the Wardrobe*, was published in 1950 while he was fellow in English at Magdalen College, Oxford. On 5 January 1951 he wrote to the book's illustrator, Pauline Baynes (1922–2008), enclosing this rough map of Narnia. It shows his vision of the area between the Wild Lands of the north and Archenland in the south. Lantern Waste lies to the north-west, Trufflehunter's Cave is in the south-west, and on the east is the sea coast. Hills, ridges, rivers and major woods are indicated and an area is marked in which marshes would be required in a future story. He asked Pauline Baynes to trick out these bare bones with mountains and castles,

ships, whales and dolphins and 'winds blowing at the corners'. Her version of the map appeared on the endpapers of the second of the Narnia chronicles, *Prince Caspian*, later in 1951. It included all Lewis's suggested improvements, including the marshes, with some further embellishments.

Pauline Baynes presented Lewis's sketch-map and his letters concerning it to the Bodleian in 1967 in response to an appeal from Walter Hooper, C.S. Lewis's secretary, who was instrumental in forming an extensive archive at the library of Lewis's manuscripts and letters.

MS. Eng. lett. c. 220, fol. 160

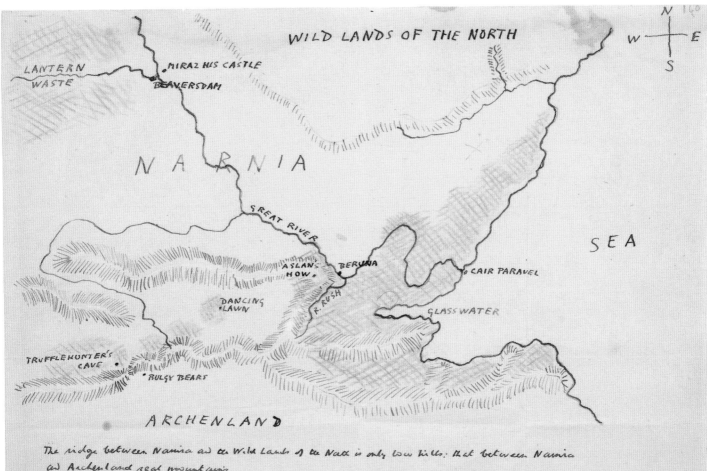

The ridge between Narnia and the Wild Lands of the North is only low hills: that between Narnia and Archenland, real mountains.

Aslan's How is on a moderate hill: but the range of which it is the Eastern end gets higher as it goes Westward.

Green = major woods.

✗ A future story will require mountains here. We needn't mark them now, but must not put in anything inconsistent with them!

The Four Seasons

This remarkable example of twentieth-century
calligraphic art was acquired from the artists by the
American book-collector and librarian Philip Hofer
and presented by him to the Bodleian Library in 1964.
Entitled *Quartet of the Seasons*, the text was chosen and
written on vellum between 1955 and 1961 by the
calligrapher and teacher Irene Wellington (1904–1984),
the decoration being designed and executed by Marie
Angel. Shown here is one of the leaves illustrating
autumn. The text is by Robert Frost.

MS. Don. d. 136 fol. 10r

216

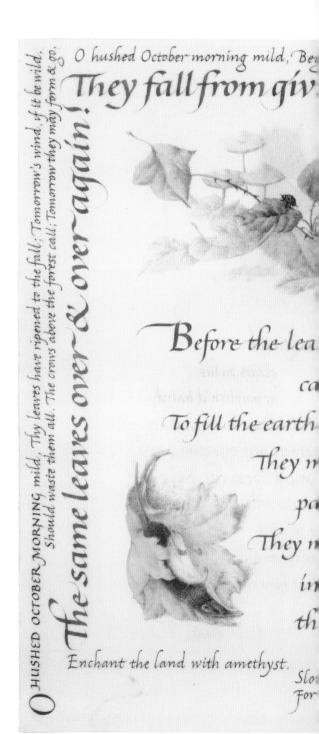

hours of this day slow. Make the day seem to us less brief. Hearts not averse to being beguiled,

shade above To make one texture of faded brown

ount again

another shade,

go down

ings coming up.

go down

rk decayed.

apes' sake, if they were all,

They must be pierced by flowers & put

Beneath the feet of dancing flowers.

However it is

in some other world

I know that this is the way in ours.

Whose leaves already are burnt with frost,
Whose clustered fruit must else be lost — For the grapes' sake along the wall.

Beguile us in the way you know. Release one leaf at break of day; At noon release another leaf; One from our trees, one far away. Retard the sun with gentle mist;

And fit the earth like a leather glove.

The Wind in the Willows

The Wind in the Willows, one of the best-loved children's books of the twentieth century and a classic of children's literature, arose from a story told by the Secretary of the Bank of England, Kenneth Grahame, to his often difficult 4-year-old son Alastair in 1904. The story about moles, water rats, a badger and a toad was continued by letter in order to keep Alastair (nicknamed Mouse) happy when Grahame and his wife were on holiday at Fowey in Cornwall in 1907, leaving him at home with his governess.

The Wind in the Willows was published in 1908. It was not well received by reviewers but rapidly became very popular both in Great Britain and the United States, where President Theodore Roosevelt personally commended the book to the publisher Charles Scribner.

Alastair's troubled childhood continued into young adulthood. Despite a limited intellectual capacity and very poor eyesight, he attended school at Rugby and Eton and entered Christ Church, Oxford, as an undergraduate in 1918. During his second year there, on 7 May 1920, he was found dead on the railway track at Port Meadow in Oxford. He was Kenneth and Elspeth Grahame's only child. Kenneth as a boy had been at school in Oxford but had been frustrated in his wish to attend Oxford University by his uncle, who acted as his guardian. On his death in 1932, however, Kenneth Grahame bequeathed to the University of Oxford 'for the benefit of the Bodleian Library' the copyright in all his works, and the continuing popularity of The Wind in the Willows enabled the library to establish a fund from its royalties for the purchase of books and manuscripts which would otherwise have been beyond its means. Subsequently, in 1943, Elspeth Grahame presented to the library the original letters to 'Mouse' and Alastair's copy of the manuscript of The Wind in the Willows. She died in 1946, and in her will bequeathed to the library the chalk drawing of Kenneth Grahame by John Singer Sargent, which is dated 1912.

Portrait of Grahame, LP 478; MS. Eng. misc. d. 281 fols. 9r–10v

TELEPHONE 0197.

The FOWEY HOTEL

FOWEY, CORNWALL, 7th June 1907.

My dearest Mouse

I hope you are having better weather than we are getting here. It is so wet & windy here that we cannot... boats, or fly kites, or sail...

You may be... further things happened... home, after his escape from... were pursuing him to to... Well, next morning the su... the hollow tree, & woke up... sleeping soundly, after his... of the previous day. He... combed the dead leaves... his fingers, & set off wal...

very cold & rather hungry. Well, he walked & he walked till he came to a canal, & he thought that must lead to a town, so he walked along the tow-path, & presently he met a horse, with a long rope attached to it, towing a barge; & he waited for the barge to come up, & there was a man steering it, & he nodded, & said 'Goodmorning, washerwoman! what are you doing here?' Then the toad made a pitiful face, & said "Please, kind Sir, I am going to pay a visit to my married daughter, who lives near a fine house called 'Toad Hall'; but I've lost my way, & spent all my money, & I'm very tired." Then the man said "Toad Hall? Why, I'm going that way myself. Jump in, & I'll give you a lift." So he steered the barge close to the bank, & the toad stepped on board & sat down, very pleased with himself. Presently the man said "I don't see why I should give you a lift for nothing, so you take that

a shirt, you very silly old woman!" Then the toad lost his temper, & quite forgot himself, & said "Don't you dare to speak to your betters like that! And don't call me a silly old woman! I'm no more an old woman than you are yourself, you common, low, vulgar bargee!" Then the bargee looked closely at him, & cried out "Why, no, I can see you're not really a washerwoman at all! You're nothing but an old toad!" Then he grabbed the toad by one hind-leg & one fore leg, & swung him round & sent him flying through the air ......

Like that - Splosh!!

He found himself head-over-ears in the water!

When the toad came to the surface he wiped the water out of his eyes & struck out for the shore; but the woman's dress he was wearing got round his legs, & made it very hard work. When at last he was safely on the tow-path again, he saw the barge disappearing in the distance, & the man looking back & laughing at him. This made Mr Toad mad with rage. He tucked the wet skirt up well under his arms, & ran as hard as he could along the path,

& passed the barge, & ran on till he overtook the horse that was towing it, and unfastened the tow-rope, & jumped on the horse's back, & dug his heels into its sides, & off they went at a gallop! He took one look back as they went, & he saw that the barge had run into the opposite bank of the canal, & stuck, & the bargee was shaking his fist at him & calling out "Stop, stop, stop!!" But the toad never stopped, but only laughed & galloped on & on & on, across country, over fields & hedges, until he had left the canal, & the barge, & the bargee, miles & miles behind him

I am afraid the Gipsy will have to wait till the next letter.

Your affectionate
Daddy

I am so glad to hear you have been out in a motor boat

The wind of change

The Bodleian Library has for the past half-century been gathering in, as research materials, the private papers of modern British politicians. It now houses a large group of such archives, including the papers of the twentieth-century prime ministers Asquith, Attlee, Macmillan, Wilson, Callaghan and Heath. Often politicians stay in the public memory for particular speeches, copies of which remain with their papers. Speeches, however, are crafted to be received aurally. They are designed to be heard rather than read. The texts which survive among modern political papers are often in typescript; though of great importance as a record, they are not very photogenic and do not make striking exhibition pieces or illustrations.

However, from time to time they can be very revealing – such is the case with that illustrated here. Perhaps the speech for which, on the international scene, Prime Minister Harold Macmillan is most remembered is that delivered on 3 February 1960 to both houses of the South African Parliament in the heartland of white rule at the close of a pan-African tour. It is known, from one phrase in it, as the 'Wind of Change' speech. The prime minister confessed in his memoirs that he was very apprehensive about delivering it. 'I had approached this ordeal with much trepidation', he wrote 'and I had taken the greatest care in the preparation of my speech.'

The draft for it survives in his papers and from it one can see that the famous words 'The wind of change is blowing throughout the continent' were not in the speech as first drafted. Macmillan had used it not long before in a speech given in Accra, Nigeria, where it had gone unremarked. Its re-employment here, however, as an afterthought to render more forceful the statement (not at all palatable to many of those in the audience) that across Africa 'whether we like it or not the growth of national consciousness is a political fact' was seized upon by the media and caused a worldwide reaction.

MS. Macmillan dep. c. 788, fol. 19 (Photograph of Harold Macmillan delivering his speech in Cape Town, 3 February 1960); MS. Macmillan dep. c. 788, fol. 155r

~~tide is now turning a little. Many nations are coming~~
~~to believe in closer association onewith another. There~~
~~is a sense of greater inter-dependence. I shall have~~
~~more to say of this later on.~~ But nationalism is not
~~confined to Europe. All over the world this century~~
~~and the past few years in particular have seen a~~
~~repetition of the process~~ which gave birth to the
~~European~~ nation states. We have seen the awakening of
national consciousness in peoples who have for
centuries lived in dependence of some other power. Today ~~this~~ is happening ~~all over~~ Africa. ~~And~~ The most
striking of all the impressions I have formed since I
left London ~~just~~ a month ago is of the strength of this
African national consciousness. In different places it
may take ~~somewhat~~ different forms. But it is happening
everywhere. Whether we like it or not ~~it~~ is a
political fact ~~of the first importance.~~ ~~We ignore it~~
~~at our peril.~~

Of course you understand this as well as anyone. You are sprung from Europe, ~~But~~ here in Africa
you have created a new nation. ~~In~~ history yours will be
the first of the African nationalisms. And ~~the~~ tide of
national consciousness which is now rising ~~all over the~~
~~continent~~ is a fact for which you and we and the other
nations of the Western world are ultimately responsible.
For its causes are to be found in the ~~successes~~ of
Western civilisation in ~~throwing~~ forward the frontiers
of knowledge, applying science in the service of human

221

-6-

Fine binding

Decoration on the binding of a book bore little relation to its contents before the nineteenth century. In the twentieth century connections between a book's covers and its text became of prime importance for commissioned work from fine binders. In 1963 the collectors Mr and Mrs Albert Ehrman commissioned Christopher Clarkson to bind a copy of F.A. Girling's *English Merchants' Marks. A field survey of marks made by Merchants and Tradesmen in England between 1400 and 1700*, which had been printed at the Royal College of Art's Lion and Unicorn Press in London in 1962. Albert Ehrman had seen and admired Christopher Clarkson's work at the Royal College's 'Graphics' exhibition in May 1963. The relationship between cover and contents is magnificently shown in the resulting binding.

Using light and dark grey goatskins over millboard, Clarkson created a different design on each cover showing a medieval town with houses made up from nineteen unit shapes placed at angles to reflect the light in varying degrees, while examples of merchants' marks are impressed in gilt on dark bands running above and below the central panel.

Christopher Clarkson subsequently became one of the world's leading experts on the conservation of books after his experience in helping to repair the ravages of the Florence flood of 1966. From 1979 to 1987 he was the Bodleian Library's chief conservation officer.

Broxb. 56.21

ENGLISH MERCHANTS MARKS

Alan Bennett

Alan Bennett (b. 1934), one of England's most successful and popular authors for the stage, screen and television in the second half of the twentieth and the early twenty-first centuries, gave his literary papers to the Bodleian Library in 2008. He is famously a member of the last generation not to use a computer, and his archive of handwritten and typescript items (the initial tranche of which fills two hundred boxes) may well be the last contemporary literary collection generated in this way to be accessioned at the library.

An Oxford graduate (he took a first-class degree in 1957 and began, but later abandoned, research for a doctorate in medieval history), Bennett is also one of that generation whose school and university education was financed from the public purse. In donating his papers he wrote, 'I say with some pride that I had a state education: school, university. None of it cost me or my parents a penny … I see this gift as some small recompense both to the university and also … to the state.' It was 'an obligation repaid'.

Alan Bennett first came to general public notice as one of the four-man team who wrote and acted in the influential satirical review *Beyond the Fringe* in 1960. His first stage play came in 1968 with *Forty Years On*, and in the following half-century many of his plays went on to win international acclaim, both on the stage and in

the cinema. These included *The Madness of George III* (1991), *Single Spies* (1998) and *The History Boys* (2004). From a large body of work for television, his monologues *Talking Heads* (1988, 1998) won the Hawthornden Prize.

Illustrated here are the papers generated in the writing of *The Lady in the Van*, published first in The London Review of Books in 1989, then as a monograph in 1990, and finally reshaped as a play for the National Theatre in 1999. The lady was the eccentric Miss Mary Teresa Sheppard (Shepherd in the play), who camped in her van in Bennett's front garden in Camden Town, London, for some fifteen years before her death in 1989, though he had been aware of her since the late 1960s as an extraordinary character who 'inhabited a different world

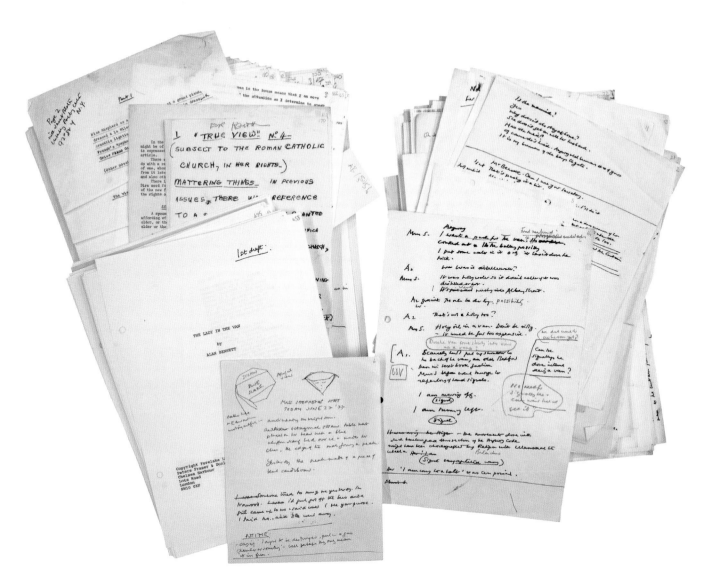

from ordinary humanity … a world in which the Virgin Mary could be encountered outside the Post Office … a world in which her advice was welcomed by world leaders and the College of Cardinals took note of her opinion.'

Particularly highlighted are two sheets showing the playwright at work: one containing notes on remarks made by Miss Sheppard together with a sketch of one of her hats improvised from a table mat, and the other an amended dialogue from Act 1 of the play featuring Miss Sheppard and two versions (A1 and A2) of the playwright himself.

MS. Bennett 156

225

Bodley's Librarians

The Bodleian Library, during the four centuries of its existence, has sought to acquire portraits of the twenty-five scholar–librarians who have directed it and held the title of Bodley's Librarian.

The first was Thomas James (1600–20), chosen as a formidable Protestant scholar by Sir Thomas Bodley himself and the first person to produce a published catalogue of the contents of any large library. The painter of his portrait is not known, though it has been attributed to Gilbert Jackson. The other three portraits reproduced here, all financed by subscription, are by very well-known painters. That of a tired Henry Octavius Coxe (1860–81) is by G.F. Watts. When it was received, it was praised as a very fine picture though not capturing the spirit of a man whom, earlier in life, Benjamin Jowett had described as 'overflowing with human kindness who charmed us all by his courtesy and grace'. Sir Edmund Craster (1931–45), during whose tenure of office the New Bodleian Library (now the Weston Library) came into being, was painted in 1944 by Augustus John. The portrait of David Vaisey (1986–96), under whom computerization was brought in to virtually all the library's processes, is the only one whose portrait also pictures part of the library's historic buildings. It is by Paul Brason.

LP 88, 308, 416, 788

Index

Concordance of shelfmarks

Copyright credits

Thanks are due to the following for permission to reproduce images in this book:

First published in 2015 by the Bodleian Library
Broad Street
Oxford OX1 3BG

www.bodleianshop.co.uk

ISBN: 978 1 85124 408 9

Text © Bodleian Library, University of Oxford, 2015
Images, unless specified above, © Bodleian Library, University of Oxford,
2015

Designed and typeset by Dot Little at the Bodleian Library
in 10/14pt Monotype Joanna
Printed and bound by Great Wall Printing Co. Ltd., Hong Kong on 128gsm
matt art paper

British Library Catalogue in Publishing Data
A CIP record of this publication is available from the British Library